THE SECOND WORLD WAR
FOUNDATION EDITION

D1556607

CONTENTS

1 APPEASEMENT: 1938–9

Key Issues

- Why did Chamberlain appease Hitler?
- Did appeasement help to cause the war?

The word '**appeasement**' means: 'giving a bully what he wants'. It is used to describe the policy of the British Prime Ministers Stanley Baldwin (1935-7) and Neville Chamberlain (1937–40) when they tried to stop a war with Germany by giving Hitler what he wanted.

THE TREATY OF VERSAILLES

Why did Chamberlain appease Hitler?

1. The First World War had been terrible, and Chamberlain did not want to cause the deaths of so many men again.
2. Many people thought that the Treaty of Versailles (made in 1919 at the end of the First World War) was unfair on Germany. The Germans hated it. Chamberlain hoped that, if he was fair with Hitler, the Germans would stop being so angry.
3. The 1930s were the time of the **Great Depression**. Chamberlain did not think that Britain could afford to spend lots of money building up her armed forces. He could only do so if he kept out of war.
4. Chamberlain was more worried about defending the British Empire in the Far East than about Germany.
5. The British public wanted peace.

THE MUNICH AGREEMENT

Bit by bit, Hitler broke the Treaty of Versailles. He built up Germany's armed forces, marched into the Rhineland (1936) and took over Austria (1938). In 1938 he demanded the Sudetenland (the part of Czechoslovakia where three million Germans lived). Czechoslovakia got ready to fight.

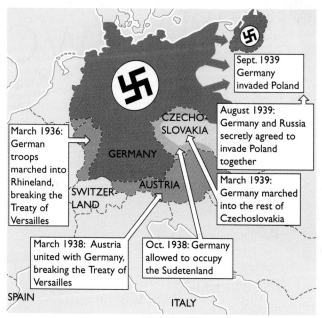

How Germany grew, 1936–9.

March 1936: German troops marched into Rhineland, breaking the Treaty of Versailles

March 1938: Austria united with Germany, breaking the Treaty of Versailles

Oct. 1938: Germany allowed to occupy the Sudetenland

March 1939: Germany marched into the rest of Czechoslovakia

August 1939: Germany and Russia secretly agreed to invade Poland together

Sept. 1939 Germany invaded Poland

At Munich in September 1938, however, Chamberlain – together with the leaders of France (Daladier) and Italy (Mussolini) – gave the Sudetenland to Hitler. The Czechs were not asked what they thought.

The Munich Agreement was appeasement in action. Many British people were happy with it (Sources D and F). But one man – Winston Churchill – said that Munich was a terrible mistake, and that it would not stop Hitler.

Churchill was right. In March 1939, Hitler's army marched into the rest of Czechoslovakia. Chamberlain and Daladier realised that Hitler could not be trusted. They thought that Hitler would next try to take over Poland. So Britain and France promised that, this time, if Hitler attacked Poland, they would go to war.

Key Words

- appeasement • Chamberlain • Baldwin • First World War • Treaty of Versailles • Great Depression • Hitler • Sudetenland • Munich • Daladier • Churchill • Poland • Nazi–Soviet Pact

The publishers would like to thank the following individuals, institutions and companies for permission to reproduce copyright illustrations in this book:

The Advertising Archive Ltd: p. 54; AKG Images: p. 28; © Bettmann/CORBIS: pp 21 (top), 23; © Corbis: p. 33; John Frost Newspaper Library: pp 15, 35 (bottom); The Hoover Institution: pp 19 (top), 26; Hulton Archive/Getty Images: pp 3, 4 (top), 7, 10, 13, 21 (bottom), 35 (top), 36, 41 (top and bottom), 43, 44, 55; © Hulton-Deutsch Collection/CORBIS: pp 4 (bottom), 12, 45 (bottom), 47 (top); with the permission of the Trustees of the Imperial War Museum, London: pp 11 'Little Ships at Dunkirk' by Norman Wilkinson (The Art Archive/© IWM), 17 (IWM UK1962), 19 (bottom) (IWM RUS 1263), 31 (top) (IWM PST 0658), 38 (IWM MH 6718), 47 (bottom) (IWM PST 3095), 49 (IWM 2892), 53 (bottom) 'A Balloon Site, Coventry' by Dame Laura Knight (IWM LD 2750), 59; David Low/*Evening Standard*/Centre for the Study of Cartoons and Caricature, University of Kent at Canterbury © Atlantic Syndication: p. 9; The National Archives: pp 45 (bottom) (INF 3/1707), 49 (top) (INF 13/144 (18)); The National Archives/HIP/Topham Picturepoint: pp 22, 53 (top); The National Archives, USA: p 31 (bottom) (111-C-5904); Peter Newark's Pictures: p. 37; Office of War Information, Washington DC: p. 27; © Popperfoto.com: p. 39; Public Record Office p. 51 (INF 3/400); © Topham Picturepoint: pp 25, 56; Vicky/News Chronicle/Centre for the Study of Cartoons and Caricature, University of Kent at Canterbury, © Atlantic Syndication: p. 57.

The publishers would also like to thank the following for permission to reproduce material in this book:

Allen Lane for the extracts from *Russia's War* by R Overy (1997); Allen & Unwin for the extracts from *The Ministry of Morale* by I McClaine (1979); Aurum Press Ltd for the extracts from *The World War II Databook* by J Ellis (1993); the BBC for the extract from the BBC history website; BBC Books for the extract from *The Battle of the Atlantic* by A Williams (2002); David Higham Associates for the extract from *Now the War is Over* by P Addison (BBC/Jonathan Cape, 1985); Bloomsbury Publishing for the extract from *Waiting for the All Clear* by B Wicks (1990); Jonathan Cape for the extracts from *Why the Allies Won* by R Overy (1995) and *Blitzkrieg* by L Deighton (1979); Century Hutchinson for the extracts from *Don't you know there is a war on?* by J Croall (1989); Collins for the extract from *The Collins Encyclopedia of Military* History by E & T Dupuy (ed) (1993); Collins and Brown for the extract from *British History* by J Gardiner & N Wenborn (ed) (1995); Coronet for the extracts from *Finest Hour* by T Clayton & P Craig (1999); Crowell for the extracts from *World War 1939–1945* by P Young (1966); The Daily Mail for the extract from *The Daily Mail* (June 1940); Granada for the extract from *Goodbye Darkness* by W Manchester (1985); Grange Books for the extract from *The Experience of World War Two* by J Campbell (ed) (1989); Grapevine/Thorsons Publishing Group for the extract from *Women at War* by S Saywell (1985); Greenhill Books for the extract from *War on the Eastern Front* by J Lucas (1991); The Guardian for the extract from *The Guardian* (October, 1938); Hamlyn for the extract from *The Military History of World War II* by B Pitt (ed) (1986); Harper Collins for the extract from For Five Shillings a Day by R Begg & P Liddle (ed) (2002); Heinemann for the extract from *The Forties by A Jenkins* (1977); Hyman Unwin for the extracts from *The Rise and Fall of the Great Powers* by P Kennedy (1988); Mandarin for the extract from *London at War* by P Ziegler (1996); Marshall Cavendish for the extract from *The War Years, 1939–45: Eyewitness Accounts* by J Lucas (1994); Methuen for the extract from *Infamy* by J Toland (1982); John Murray for the extract from *An Underworld at War* by D Thomas (2003); the extracts from *The Oxford Companion to the Second World War* by I C B Dear (Gen. ed) (1995), the extract from *The USA, 1917–1980* by N Smith (1996) and the extract from *Britain and Europe* by J Joll (ed) (1967) by permission of Oxford University Press; Pan for the extract from *The First Casualty* by P Knightly (1975); Penguin for the extracts from *Total War* by P Calvocoressi (1972) and *Britain in the Modern World* by E Nash & A Newth (1967); Readers Digest for the extract from *Life on the Home Front* by T Healey (1993); The Spectator for the extract from *The Spectator* (September, 1940); Thames Methuen for the extracts from *A People's War* by P Lewis (1986); Thames Television for the material from *A People's War* (1986) (a Thames Television programme); Triad Panther for the extract from *Fighter* by L Deighton (1979); William Morrow for the extract from *Barbarossa* by A Clark (1965); Viking for the extracts from *Stalingrad* by A Beevor (1998); Virago Books for the extract from *Hearts Undefeated* by J Hartley (ed) (1994).

All sources have been adapted to make them more accessible to students.

Every effort has been made to trace and acknowledge ownership of copyright. The publishers will be glad to make suitable arrangements with any copyright holders whom it has not been possible to contact.

Note about the Internet links in the book. The user should be aware that URLs or web addresses change regularly. Every effort has been made to ensure the accuracy of the URLs provided in this book on going to press. It is inevitable, however, that some will change. It is sometimes possible to find a relocated web page, by just typing in the address of the home page for a website in the URL window of your browser.

Artwork by Art Construction.

Orders: please contact Bookpoint Ltd, 130 Milton Park, Abingdon, Oxon OX14 4SB. Telephone: (44) 01235 827720. Fax: (44) 01235 400454. Lines are open from 9.00 – 6.00, Monday to Saturday, with a 24 hour message answering service. You can also order through our website www.hodderheadline.co.uk

British Library Cataloguing in Publication Data
A catalogue record for this title is available from the British Library

ISBN 0 340 814 225

First Published   2004
Impression number 10 9 8 7 6 5 4 3 2 1
Year   2010 2009 2008 2007 2006 2005 2004

Copyright © John D. Clare 2004

Cover image shows *Give 'Em Both Barrels*, poster by Jean Carlu, 1942 © Swim Inc/CORBIS.
Typeset by Fakenham Photosetting Limited, Fakenham, Norfolk
Printed in Dubai for Hodder & Stoughton Educational, a division of Hodder Headline, 338 Euston Road, London NW1 3BH by Oriental Press.

THE NAZI–SOVIET PACT

Hitler was not worried about Chamberlain and Daladier – he despised them. But he was worried about Russia. As a Nazi, he wanted to destroy **Communist** Russia, but he did not feel strong enough to fight the Russians yet. So, on 23 August 1939, Hitler made a treaty with Russia. Nobody could believe it at the time – Nazi Germany allying with Communist Russia! In public, they promised only not to attack each other. Secretly, they agreed to divide Poland between them.

A SOURCE

This is what Winston Churchill said about the Munich Agreement of October 1938.

This is a total defeat. The government has let Germany build up its armed forces, but it has not built up our armed forces in time. So our defences are not good enough. If Hitler decides to attack us, England and France will bitterly wish they still had the strong army of Czechoslovakia.

Do not think that this is the end. This is only the beginning.

B SOURCE

In 1967 the historians E Nash and A Newth said this about the Munich Agreement.

Chamberlain gave Hitler everything he wanted. Millions of Czech people and a huge army were handed over to Germany. Nobody ever trusted France again. And although Britain built up her armed forces during 1938–1939, we did not add as much as the Czech army that had been thrown away at Munich.

C SOURCE

Appeasement – from a modern history book (1995).
Linked with Neville Chamberlain, appeasement was cowardly. Smaller and weaker countries were given to Germany to try to stop a war. At the same time, Britain did not re-arm, so Britain was almost defeated at the start of the war in 1940.

D SOURCE

How the *Guardian* newspaper (1 October 1938) described Chamberlain's return from Germany.

He drove to Buckingham Palace to meet the king and queen, and came out with them to meet the crowds. For three minutes everyone shouted 'Neville', while he stood there smiling and waving.

E SOURCE

The numbers of planes built, 1936–9 (from a modern textbook).

	1936	1937	1938	1939
France	890	743	1382	3163
Britain	1877	2153	2827	7940
Germany	5112	5606	5235	8295

F SOURCE

The crowd outside 10 Downing Street cheers Chamberlain after his return from Munich.

Questions

a What can you learn from Source A about Churchill's views on the Munich Agreement?

b Does Source C support the evidence of Sources A and B about appeasement?

c How useful are Sources D and E as evidence of the success of appeasement?

d 'Chamberlain's policy of appeasement towards Germany was the right policy at the time.' Use the sources and your own knowledge to explain whether you agree.

→ **Key Issue**

• What were the main events of the war?

RAF cadets training in 1942. The RAF was not quite as badly equipped as this! In fact, they are learning to fly in formation.

Like a football match, the Second World War was a war of two halves.

From 1939–42, the **Axis** powers (Germany, Italy and Japan) did well, and almost won the war.

From 1942–45, the **Allied powers** (Britain, Russia and America) did better, and went on to win the war.

This chapter tells you the main events of the war.

YEARS OF AXIS VICTORY

At first, the Axis powers did very well.

<u>September 1939</u>: Germany had invented a new way of attacking, called *Blitzkrieg* ('lightning war'), and the German army easily defeated Poland. At the same time, the Russian army took over eastern Poland.

<u>April 1940</u>: after a time of quiet, called the '**phoney war**', Hitler invaded Norway, to make sure Germany would get iron ore.

<u>May 1940</u>: Hitler's next step was to invade and conquer France. The British army which had gone to France was surrounded at Dunkirk and lost all its equipment – although 330,000 British and French troops escaped back to Britain.

<u>August–September 1940</u>: 'the Battle of Britain' – the German *Luftwaffe* (airforce) tried to defeat Britain's Royal Air Force, but failed. After September 1940, the Germans began night-bombing raids (known as 'the **Blitz**'), first of London, then of other British cities, which lasted until May 1941.

INVASION OF RUSSIA

<u>June 1941</u>: although Hitler had not conquered Britain, he thought that Britain was all but defeated, so he invaded Russia. Three million German soldiers invaded Russia. At first they easily defeated the Russian armies. By October 1941, the Germans were only 100 km from Moscow.

WORLD AT WAR

After taking over eastern Poland, Russia invaded Finland (November 1939). In the end, the Russian army defeated Finland (March 1940), but it did so badly that Hitler thought it would be easy to defeat Russia, and this tempted him to invade Russia in June 1941.

<u>December 1941</u>: the war became a World War when Japan made a surprise attack on the American navy base at Pearl Harbor. Japan, Germany and Italy declared war on America.

The Japanese then attacked British forces in the Far East. At first, they did very well, and in February 1942 they captured Singapore.

About the same time, the Italians invaded North Africa. At first, the British army there managed to defeat them, but then Hitler sent troops to help the Italians and the British were defeated again.

YEARS OF ALLIED TRIUMPH

After 1942, the Allies began to win the war.

North Africa: the British defeated the Germans at the battle of El Alamein (November 1942). In July 1943, Allied forces invaded Italy, and in September 1943 the Italian army surrendered.

Russia: after a huge battle, the Russians destroyed the German Sixth Army at Stalingrad (January 1943). They then defeated the Germans at Kursk (July 1943) in the biggest tank-battle in history. After that, they drove the Germans back, and it was the Russians who captured Berlin in April 1945.

Normandy: in June 1944, Allied forces invaded France (the 'D-Day' landings). In August 1944 they 'liberated' (freed) Paris from the Nazis. But the Allies found it hard to advance into Germany. A British attack on Arnhem (September 1944) was defeated. And the Germans made an unsuccessful counter-attack at the 'Battle of the Bulge' (December 1944).

Key Words
- Sept 1939: Poland – phoney war
- May 1940: France – Battle of Britain
- June 1941: Russia
- Dec 1941: Pearl Harbor
- June 1942: Midway
- Nov 1942: El Alamein
- Jan 1943: Stalingrad
- 6 June 1944: D-Day
- 8 May 1945: VE Day
- 6 Aug 1945: Hiroshima
- 15 Aug 1945: VJ Day

VE Day: In April 1945 the Russians captured Berlin. Hitler shot himself. Germany surrendered on 8 May 1945 – 'Victory in Europe' Day (VE Day).

THE WAR IN THE PACIFIC

In June 1942 the American navy defeated the Japanese navy at the battle of Midway. In 1944, the American navy won two more important sea-battles, and the American army began taking over key Japanese islands in the Pacific. In April 1945, the Americans captured the island of Okinawa, which was close enough to invade Japan.

But invading Japan would mean the deaths of thousands of American soldiers. So, instead of invading Japan, the Americans dropped atomic bombs on Hiroshima (6 August 1945) and Nagasaki (9 August 1945).

Japan surrendered on 15 August 1945 – 'Victory in Japan' Day (VJ Day).

Question

Read through this chapter and then copy and complete the chart below. List all of the key dates of each important event in the war from 1939–43. The dates in 1939 have already been listed. Complete the second and third columns for each date you have listed.

Date	Description	Victory for
September 1939	Germany invaded Poland	Germany

Write a summary account of the war in no more than 80 words, under these headings:
- Years of defeat, 1939–40
- The Turning Point: the invasion of Russia
- Victory in Europe, 1942–45
- Victory in the Pacific, 1942–45

Concentrate on developments, not events.

3 BLITZKRIEG

Key Issue
- Why was *Blitzkrieg* so successful?

Key Words
- *Blitzkrieg* • surprise • dive bombers
- paratroopers • tanks • soldiers in trucks
- Maginot Line

Hitler had a small well-trained, very modern army. But he had to win the war quickly – he did not have enough weapons or supplies to fight a long war. So the German army invented the idea of '**Blitzkrieg**' ('lightning war').

SURPRISE IS THE KEY

The most important thing about a *blitzkrieg* attack was surprise. When the German army attacked Poland in 1939 most of the Polish airforce was completely unprepared and the German planes were able to destroy the Polish planes on the runways. Hitler's attack on France in 1940 was made at a place the French were not expecting, and his attack on Russia in 1941 was a surprise also.

WHAT HAPPENED IN A *BLITZKRIEG* ATTACK?

1. A German *blitzkrieg* attack started with dive bomber attacks. This caused panic and jammed up the roads, as frightened enemy civilians tried to get out of the area.
2. At the same time, German paratroopers dropped behind enemy lines, attacking enemy command centres, telephone exchanges and bridges. The enemy generals

found themselves unable to send orders or organise a counter-attack.
3. Then large numbers of tanks attacked weak points in the enemy line, followed up by huge numbers of soldiers in trucks. The Germans did not even try to capture enemy strong-points, but went round them. Enemy soldiers found themselves cut off from their supplies, and they had to surrender.

SUCCESSFUL TACTICS

The German army in 1940 was smaller than the British and French. It had fewer tanks than the British and French, and the **Allied** tanks were better than the German tanks.

A SOURCE

In 1979 General Nehring, a German general who fought in the battle of France, remembered the following.

In 1940, the French Army was the most powerful in the world. The French had more tanks and more men than the Germans. But they did not have any new ideas. Although they had seen Blitzkrieg tactics in Poland, they thought the Maginot Line would save them.

B SOURCE

A map showing the German attack on France and the Maginot Line.

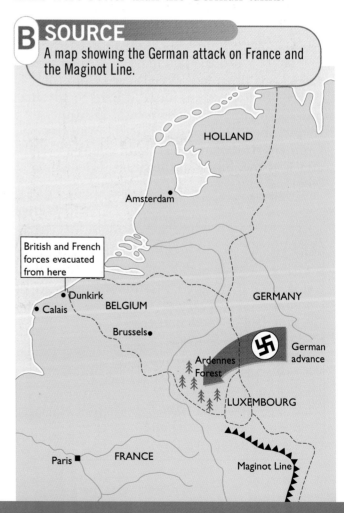

HOLLAND

Amsterdam

British and French forces evacuated from here

Dunkirk
Calais
BELGIUM
Brussels
GERMANY

Ardennes Forest

German advance

LUXEMBOURG

Paris
FRANCE

Maginot Line

WHY WERE *BLITZKRIEG* TACTICS SO SUCCESSFUL AT THE START OF THE WAR?

1. They were good tactics, and they took the out-of-date Allied generals by surprise. The French put their hopes in the Maginot Line (a huge complex of tunnels, railways and artillery – a super-version of a World War One trench).
2. The Allied generals did not understand how to use tanks. They used them in small numbers to protect their soldiers (as in the First World War). The Germans used them in large numbers as an attacking force.
3. The Germans were the attackers – they chose where they were going to attack, so they could attack altogether. The Allies had to spread out their forces to try to defend everywhere at once.
4. The Germans had many more airplanes.

C SOURCE

From a modern history book (1999).

The Maginot Line was supposed to be unbeatable. It was very strong from Switzerland to Belgium.

But north from that it was just pillboxes and barbed wire, put in quickly in the winter of 1939. The Germans easily smashed through it.

E SOURCE

The armed forces in France, Britain and Germany in May 1940.

	Aircraft	Tanks
France	1368	3063
Britain	456	310
Germany	4020	2445

F SOURCE

From a modern history book (1990).

The French army had lots of men and tanks, but the French generals had not understood the idea of fighting together in large numbers (as the Germans had done in Poland).

The French soldiers were spread out thinly all along the Maginot Line.

D SOURCE

French troops digging trenches near the Maginot Line in 1940.

Questions

a What can you learn from Source A about Allied military thinking in 1940?

b Does Source C support the evidence of Sources A and B about the German invasion of France in 1940?

c How useful are Sources D and E as evidence about why France was defeated in 1940?

d 'Germany's success in 1940 was due to better weapons and better tactics.' Use the sources and your own knowledge to explain whether you agree with this view.

4 GERMAN ADVANCES: 1939–40

Key Issue

- Why did the Allies lose so many battles at the start of the war?

Key Words
- Poland • phoney war • '*Sitzkrieg*'
- Norway • Churchill
- 'blood, toil, tears and sweat'
- Holland, Belgium, France
- Dunkirk • 47 days

THE DEFEAT OF POLAND

The German army invaded Poland on 1 September 1939. On 17 September 1939, the Russians also invaded Poland, from the east (as agreed in the Nazi–Soviet Pact in August).

Britain and France declared war on Germany on 3 September 1939, but did nothing else. The Polish army tried to fight back. But it got no help from Britain and France – they could have attacked Germany from the west, but they chose not to do so. Poland was alone, and was easily defeated.

THE PHONEY WAR

So, for the first seven months of the war (September 1939–April 1940), the British did nothing. People called it the '**phoney war**', and made jokes about '*Sitzkrieg*'.

They were soon punished for this. In April 1940, Germany invaded and conquered Norway. The British and French sent troops to help Norway, but they were easily defeated.

One good thing did come out of the fall of Norway. Chamberlain resigned, and Winston Churchill became Prime Minister. Churchill had always opposed **appeasement**, and attacked the government's half-hearted efforts during the phoney war. Now Britain had a leader who would do anything that was needed to win the war. The first thing he did was to take Conservative, Labour and Liberal politicians into the government. Later, he made alliances with **communists**, bombed cities and sacrificed soldiers. He promised the British people: 'blood, toil, tears and sweat'.

THE INVASION OF FRANCE

At first, however, things got worse, not better. In May 1940, the Germans invaded Holland, Belgium, and then France.

France was Hitler's greatest victory. Hitler forced his generals – who would have been more careful – to attack.

The French thought that the Maginot Line would stop the Germans.

But Hitler did not attack the Maginot Line. This was because he knew that the Maginot Line only protected the border between France and Germany. The French had not built any strong defences along the border with Belgium. They thought that the forests in the Ardennes area were too thick to allow a big attack.

They were wrong. It was there that Hitler attacked.

The German army at this time was the best in the world. It destroyed the **Allied** defences. During the attack, hundreds of thousands of British and French soldiers became cut off at the port of Dunkirk.

It took the German army only 47 days to conquer France.

A **SOURCE**

In 1986 the historian Peter Lewis wrote this about the early years of the war.

The RAF dropped leaflets, not bombs, on Germany. When an MP suggested fire-bombing the Black Forest, the government got angry: 'It would burn down people's houses!'

B SOURCE

In 1986, the historian Barrie Pitt wrote this about Chamberlain's government in the early years of the war.

The government dropped 18 million leaflets, telling Germans how wicked Hitler was. But it insisted that no damage at all could be done to German buildings, in case it annoyed the Germans.

C SOURCE

In 1966 the historian Peter Young wrote this about the early years of the war.

Britain could have helped Poland by bombing German cities. But even Churchill said this would be a mistake – he thought the Americans would not like it if Britain bombed Germany before Germany bombed Britain. So the RAF dropped leaflets.

D SOURCE

This cartoon, 'Very well, alone', is from the *London Evening Standard* newspaper, 18 June 1940. It shows the attitude of the British press, under Churchill's influence, after the fall of France.

E SOURCE

From a speech by Winston Churchill, 4 June 1940.

We shall go on to the end. … We shall defend our island, whatever the cost may be. We shall fight on the beaches, we shall fight on the landing grounds, we shall fight in the fields and in the streets, we shall fight in the hills; we shall never surrender.

F SOURCE

In 1979 the historian Ian McLain wrote this about British **morale** at the start of the war.

Ministry of Information surveys between September 1939 and May 1940 found that the British people did not want to stop the war against Germany, but morale was low. People were bored and fed up. They had gone to war to defend Poland – and the government had just stood by and watched Germany crush Poland.

Questions

a What can you learn from Source A about the Chamberlain government's policy in the early stages of the war?

b Does Source C support the evidence of Sources A and B about the government's policy in the early stages of the war?

c How useful are Sources D and E as evidence of the state of public morale in the first eight months of the war?

d 'The first nine months of the war were a disaster for Britain.' Use the sources and your own knowledge to explain whether you agree with this view.

Controversy!

'Austria, Czechoslovakia, Poland, Denmark, Norway, Holland, Belgium, France – all conquered. If Hitler had stopped in May 1940, he would have gone down in history as one of the greatest rulers of all time.'

What is your INSTANT REACTION?

5 DUNKIRK AND THE BEF: 1940

Key Issue

- Was Dunkirk a miracle or a disaster?

The German attack on France in May 1940 left 250,000 British soldiers trapped in Dunkirk. The British government hoped to save 50,000 of them. In the end, between 26 May and 3 June 1940, 'Operation Dynamo' (as it was called) took out 225,000 British and 110,000 French solders. British newspapers called it 'the miracle of Dunkirk'. This has led to the '**myth**' of Dunkirk – the belief that Dunkirk was a success, not a failure.

MIRACLE ...

1. Hitler ordered his tanks to stop, and left the German airforce (the **Luftwaffe**) to finish off the battle. However, the RAF managed to fight off the *Luftwaffe*.
2. Most of the **evacuation** was done at night, when the *Luftwaffe* were not flying.
3. The British public helped. Many small boats sailed across the Channel to save the soldiers – thankfully, the weather was good.
4. 30,000 French soldiers defended Dunkirk while the British got out.

... OR DISASTER

1. The British lost huge amounts of weapons – 475 tanks and 1000 artillery guns.
2. The French felt betrayed. Britain had left them to the Germans. Churchill refused to send 120 Spitfires to France – he knew he would need them for the coming Battle of Britain. At first, the British also refused to take any French soldiers out of Dunkirk, until the French complained. Yet all this time the French were defending Dunkirk so the British could get out.

Churchill and the newspapers 'talked up' the evacuation to keep up public **morale**. But in many ways, Dunkirk was a disaster – 'wars are not won by evacuations' admitted Churchill in private.

France surrendered on 22 June 1940.

Hitler took over northern France, but left the rest of France (called **Vichy France**, after the town where the new government set up) under the control of a puppet government led by Marshall Petain.

(Hitler did the same in Norway, where a Norwegian Nazi called Vidkun Quisling took over the government.)

A SOURCE

The *Daily Mail* newspaper interviewed soldiers getting back to Britain for this report on 1 June 1940.

A gunner told me that thousands of men had spent two days on the sand, with little food and no shelter from the German dive bombers. But they had joked and played games to keep their spirits up.

A sailor told me that his ship had been sunk trying to help the trapped soldiers. But as soon as he got back to England, he and his friends all asked to go back to Dunkirk to try again.

B SOURCE

British troops return from Dunkirk. One soldier shows off a captured German gun.

C SOURCE

This picture was painted by Norman Wilkinson, a government war artist. Note the Royal Navy ships, but also the London barges, a white yacht and tugs towing lifeboats full of soldiers.

D SOURCE

From a modern history book (1999).

Although many ships were lost, the evacuation was a great success. A third of a million men had been brought home while the enemy attacked. Only about 30,000 – mostly French soldiers – had been captured.

Key Words

- Operation Dynamo • 225,000 British soldiers • 110,000 French soldiers
  • *Luftwaffe* • small boats
  • 475 tanks, 1000 artillery guns
  • betrayed • Vichy France • Petain

Questions

a What does Source A tell us about the evacuation from Dunkirk?

b Why were photographs like Source B officially approved at the time? Use Source B and your own knowledge to answer this question.

c How useful is Source C to an historian studying the evacuation from Dunkirk in 1940? Use Source C and your own knowledge to answer this question.

d Is Source D an accurate interpretation of the evacuation from Dunkirk? Use Source D and your own knowledge to answer this question.

6 THE BATTLE OF BRITAIN

Key Issue

- Why did Hitler not invade Britain?

Key Words

- Operation Sealion • Royal Navy • RAF 800 fighter planes • Dowding • free French • Spitfire • Hurricane • *Luftwaffe* • Goering • shipping • airfields • pilots • 7 September 1940 • 'Blitz' • 15 September 1940 • blackout • radar

CONTROLLING THE SKIES

After the fall of France, Hitler offered the British government a peace treaty. Some people – such as Neville Chamberlain – wanted to talk to him; they thought Britain could never win a war with Germany. But Winston Churchill would not give up, and the war went on.

If Hitler was going to conquer Britain, he would have to cross the English Channel. He code-named the German invasion: 'Operation Sealion'. But first he would have to defeat the RAF. If the RAF survived, it would be able to attack the German boats as they crossed the Channel. If he destroyed it, the *Luftwaffe* would be able to defend the German boats against the British Royal Navy.

Fighter pilots 'scramble' for their planes to meet a Luftwaffe *attack. These planes are Spitfires, but Hurricane planes were also important. These pilots are 'free French' – French pilots who had escaped from France in June 1940.*

The British government set a 'blackout' so the German planes would not know where to drop their bombs.   But there were many accidents in the dark. The white line down the pavement in this photo is to help stop people bumping into each other.

So the RAF and the *Luftwaffe* fought the Battle of Britain, from July to September 1940, to see who would control the skies.   This battle decided whether an invasion would take place or not.   Just 800 RAF fighter planes stood between Britain and defeat.

GOERING'S STRATEGY

First, the *Luftwaffe* attacked British ships in the Channel – Goering, the *Luftwaffe* commander, hoped that the British would use up fighter planes defending the ships.   Air Chief Marshall Dowding, commander of the RAF, however, refused to send any planes, so Goering had to try another plan.

In the middle of August, the *Luftwaffe* attacked British airfields.   The Germans did not destroy many planes, but they did damage the runways so planes could not take off.   Planes were easy to replace – the factories were making 500 a week.   But as the *Luftwaffe* attacks went on, more and more RAF pilots were killed, and they could not be replaced.   As time went on, the *Luftwaffe* was winning the battle.

Nevertheless, by the beginning of September, Hitler was beginning to get angry.   Goering had promised him a quick victory, and it seemed no nearer.

7 SEPTEMBER 1940

7 September 1940 was the turning point in the Battle of Britain.

At the end of August, British bombers had attacked Berlin. So Hitler told Goering to change tactics and bomb London, which they did almost every night until November 1940.

Hitler thought that 'the **Blitz**', as it came to be called, would frighten the British into surrender. But the change in tactics helped the RAF. It let the RAF repair the runways and planes, and gave the pilots a rest.

On 15 September 1940, the Germans sent 1000 bombers and 700 fighter planes to attack London.

The RAF was ready for them. There was a huge battle and the RAF won – the British claimed to have shot down 185 German planes. It did not matter that they had only shot down 60 – the British thought they had won a huge victory, and public **morale** went sky-high.

SEALION POSTPONED

In all, during the Battle of Britain, the RAF lost 800 planes, and the *Luftwaffe* lost 1300. On 17 September 1940 Hitler called off Operation Sealion.

WHY DID THE RAF WIN THE BATTLE OF BRITAIN?

1. The Spitfire was better than any of the German planes.
2. *Luftwaffe* fighter planes only had enough fuel for 20 minutes' flight time over Britain before they had to turn back.
3. The *Luftwaffe* never tried to destroy the radar stations as they did the airfields. But radar told the British when and where the German were attacking.
4. The Germans' change of tactics in September 1940 gave the RAF a chance.
5. Some historians think that Hitler never really wanted to conquer Britain anyway. He thought – although he had not conquered Britain – that Britain was not a danger any more. So he turned away to attack Russia.

A SOURCE

In 1979 the British novelist Len Deighton wrote this about the RAF base at Manston in August 1940.

The airmen had stayed in the shelters since the German attack of 12 August. The terrified men refused to go and fight. And while they were there, local people stole RAF tools and spares from the bombed buildings.

B SOURCE

From the British weekly newspaper, *The Spectator*, 13 September 1940.

*The Germans hope to break our spirit. They will fail. First they attacked our ships – but our **convoys** still go safely on their way. Then they bombed our airfields – it worked in Poland, but all our airfields are still working. And they have failed to stop our ports and dockyards.*

Controversy!

'"Never, in the field of human conflict, was so much owed by so many to so few."
Churchill may have been inspiring, but he was wrong. The RAF did not win the Battle of Britain – Hitler threw victory away.'

What is your INSTANT REACTION?

THE DAILY MAIL, Monday, September 16, 1940.

Daily Mail

FOR KING AND EMPIRE

LATE WAR NEWS SPECIAL

NO. 13,852 * * * MONDAY, SEPTEMBER 16, 1940 ONE PENNY

165 (and more) DOWN

MORE than 165 German 'planes and at least 330 airmen were shot down in the morning and afternoon attacks on London yesterday.

The R.A.F. lost 30 machines and 20 airmen.

In addition, German losses include:

18 on Saturday

Million Cheer London Battle

By Daily Mail Raid Reporters

HUNDREDS of German 'planes attempted to raid London, the Thames Estuary, and towns in the South-east yesterday—and they suffered their biggest defeat of the Blitzkrieg at the hands of our defences.

London had revelled in a "quiet night."

There was an alarm for only two hours in the middle of the night, but most people slept through it to the sooth-

GREATEST DAY FOR RAF

'Massed' Fighters in Action

INVASION FLEET IS CRIPPLED

By NOEL MONKS, Daily Mail Air Correspondent

THE German Air Force returned to mass daylight raids on the Thames estuary and attempted to smash through to the London area yesterday, only to run into the greatest concentration of Spitfires and Hurricanes ever seen over this area.

The results were devastating, for German losses up to last evening were 165 'planes and at least 330 airmen.

On Saturday night the R.A.F. gave the invasion ports their most severe battering to date.

The ports of Antwerp, Ostend, Flushing, Dunkirk, Calais, and Boulogne were heavily bombed by strong forces.

Supply depots at Osnabruck, Mannheim, Aachen, Hamm, Krefeld, and Brussels were attacked, and also rail communications.

Pilots and crews pressed home attacks in spite of severe weather. Gun emplacements at Cap Gris Nez and enemy aerodromes were also bombed.

It is considered in R.A.F. circles that at least a quarter of Hitler's invasion fleet of barges and supply ships have been written off as a result of our bombing attacks on the Channel ports.

This may not stop the invasion attempt, scheduled to start any day, but it must have caused serious dis-organisation and confusion.

As an added hazard for London's night raiders, a new type of balloon barrage has been added to our

Palace Bombed Again

RAIDER WRECKED

By Daily Mail Reporter

BUCKINGHAM PALACE was bombed again yesterday for the third time, when two heavy bombs and a number of incendiaries were dropped in a daylight attack.

The King and Queen were not in the palace. The heavy bombs which fell failed to explode—and the raider was shot to pieces by Spitfires a few seconds after the attack.

One of the crew baled out, but his parachute did not open, and he crashed on a roof.

GREEN to RED FOR 'GAS'

WEST DOOR

26 FT. DOWN

THIS Daily Mail picture-diagram shows the task that faced the St. Paul's bomb squad. You can see the direction in which the bomb was slipping, 26ft. down, threatening the Cathedral more and more each moment.

3-Day Battle with Time-Bomb

6 ENGINEERS HAVE SAVED ST. PAUL'S

By Daily Mail Reporter

A LITTLE party of Royal Engineers—an officer and five men—have saved St. Paul's Cathedral from terrible damage and possible destruction by a German time-bomb which fell from a 'plane on Thursday and buried itself 26ft. deep in a crater near the walls.

Yesterday at noon, after three days' continuous work, the bomb was secured by steel tackle and hauled to the surface with a pulley and cable attached to a lorry.

A City fireman who had been on duty continuously in the area told me :

"There were five of them, all young fellows, officered by a French-Canadian. One was an Irishman and a couple came from Yorkshire. Another, I believe, came from Lancashire.

"On the first day they couldn't start work because a gas-main, broken by the bomb, was blazing. But they've been here from early morning till dusk ever since.

"It was wonderful to watch. They used no scaffolding or supports, and there was a risk of the road falling in at any moment.

"After digging through gravel and sand they came to black mud. The bomb was still slipping along through this almost horizontally, and in 24 hours it would have tunnelled under the Cathedral steps.

"But at last they got it. I heard one of them shout down the crater, 'Have you got it yet?'—and at last the answer, 'Yes. Here it is! Listen !'.

Leon Blum Arrested

VICHY, Sunday.—M. Leon Blum, the former French Premier and Socialist leader, has been arrested, it was announced here to-day.

M. Blum was Premier in 1936 of the first Popular Front Government in France.

He is 67, a Jew, and an uncompromising opponent of Nazism.—B.U.P.

". Captives May Not Meet !—Back Page.

Westminster Abbey Hit

The west window of Westminster Abbey was slightly damaged during a recent air-raid.

"The damage was very slight, and only a few small squares were broken," said an official.

LATEST

175 DOWN

In addition to 171 German 'planes shot down yesterday up to 10 p.m. by fighters, four were brought down by anti-aircraft fire.

BOMBS ON CENTRAL LONDON

Early raiders last night did not stop to encircle London. Defi ... the A.A. barrage, they cut straight across London at great height and top speed. They dropped several bombs in Central London.

Bomb hit one of London's oldest hospitals. Doctor was injured, but patients were safe in basement.

D SOURCE

In 2002, a New Zealand pilot who fought in the Battle of Britain said the following.

We would not have survived if Hitler had not made the mistake of turning his attacks from the airfields to bombing London. It gave us a chance to get some sleep.

Make brief notes under the following headings:
- Controlling the skies
- Goering's strategy
- 7 September 1940
- Why Germany failed

Questions

a What does Source A tell us about British morale in August 1940?

b Use Source B and your own knowledge to explain why this article was published in September 1940.

c How useful is Source C as evidence of the Battle of Britain? Use Source C and your own knowledge to answer this question.

d Is Source D a fair interpretation of why Hitler failed to defeat the RAF in 1940? Use Source D and your own knowledge to answer this question.

7 THE BATTLE OF THE ATLANTIC

Key Words
- food • raw materials • U-boats • Doenitz
- wolf-packs • 'happy times'
- 'the U-boat peril' • convoys • sonar
- depth charges • Liberators

THE ATLANTIC LIFELINE

In 1939, Britain **imported** half its food and two-thirds of its **raw materials**. Hitler ordered his U-boats to sink **merchant ships** sailing to Britain. He knew that – if he could stop food and raw materials getting there – Britain would lose the war.

'THE HAPPY TIMES'

When war broke out the Germans had 22 U-boats, commanded by Admiral Karl Doenitz. By 1942, they had 300 U-boats.

In the early years of the war, the U-boats were very successful. Doenitz ordered his U-boats to hunt in large groups called 'wolf-packs'. Britain lost 1875 ships between 1940–41, a quarter of her merchant fleet. As a result, in 1941, Britain only imported a third of what was needed.

When America entered the war in 1941, American ships in the Pacific were also easy targets, lit up by the lights from the shore.

German U-boat crews called these years 'the happy times'. Nearly 1200 British and American ships were sunk in 1942 and by January 1943 the Royal Navy had only two months' supply of oil left.

'The only thing that ever frightened me in the war,' wrote Churchill, 'was the U-boat peril'.

A SOURCE

The 'Atlantic gap' was the 1000 km in the middle of the ocean where planes could not protect the ships until May 1943.

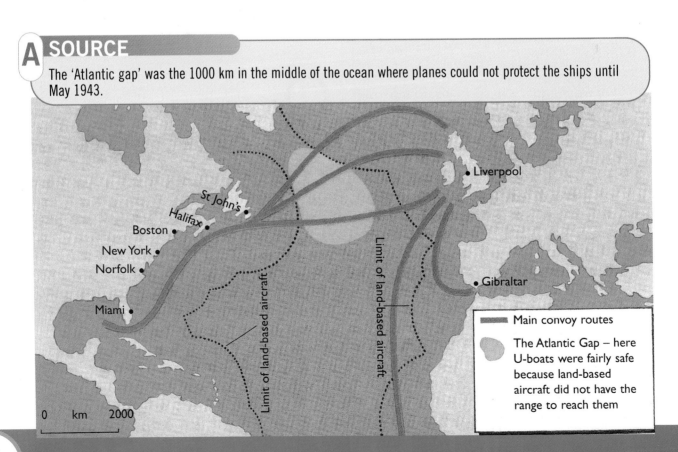

Liverpool

St John's
Halifax
Boston
New York
Norfolk

Miami

Gibraltar

Limit of land-based aircraft

Limit of land-based aircraft

0   km   2000

▬▬▬ Main convoy routes

The Atlantic Gap – here U-boats were fairly safe because land-based aircraft did not have the range to reach them

ANTI-SUBMARINE METHODS

Something had to be done, and the British found a number of ways to defeat the U-boats:

1. Merchant ships travelled in **convoys**, protected by anti-submarine warships called destroyers.
2. Destroyers used a *so*und *na*vigation *r*anging system called 'sonar' which used an echo 'ping' to find out where the U-boats were, and how deep they were.
3. When the destroyers found a U-boat, they dropped depth charges that could be set to explode at the right depth.
4. U-boats needed to come to the surface once a day to refresh the air, and to re-charge the electric motors. They did this at night. After 1943, **Allied** planes were fitted with a radar system which could pick up a U-boat 6 kms away.
5. After 1943, long-range **Liberator** airplanes were able to patrol the whole of the Atlantic, looking for U-boats.
6. After 1943, also, the British and American shipyards produced ships faster than the U-boats could sink them.

THE 'U-BOAT PERIL' ENDS

As a result of all these tactics, the tide turned. After 1943, the Allies began to win the Battle of the Atlantic.

In 1944, the U-boats sank only 117 ships – but 251 U-boats were lost sinking them. The Germans built 1100 U-boats during the war. Of these, 785 were sunk and 28,000 crewmen (72%) were killed.

B SOURCE

A British wartime poster.

A FEW
**CARELESS WORDS
MAY END IN THIS–**
Many lives were lost in the last war through careless talk
Be on your guard! Don't discuss movements of ships or troops

C SOURCE

Allied merchant ships sunk, 1939–1944.

	Tonnes	Number of ships
1939	755 000	220
1940	3 650 000	1007
1941	3 300 000	875
1942	6 150 000	1170
1943	2 170 000	363
1944	500 000	117

D SOURCE

In 2002 the modern historian David Syrett wrote this about the Battle of the Atlantic.

The Germans lost because the Allies had better tactics, and better technology.

Questions

a What does Source A tell you about the Battle of the Atlantic?
b Why were posters like Source B distributed in Britain? Use Source B and your own knowledge to answer this question.
c How useful is Source C to an historian studying the Battle of the Atlantic?
d Is Source D an accurate interpretation of why the Allies won the Battle of the Atlantic? Use Source E and your own knowledge to answer this question.

8 OPERATION BARBAROSSA

Key Issue

→ Why did Hitler invade Russia?

Key Words
- Operation Barbarossa • wheat and oil
- *lebensraum* • Aryans • Communists
- Finland • 'scorched earth'
- Russian factories • encirclement
- AGN • AGC • AGS • winter

On 22 June 1941, Hitler invaded Russia – codename: 'Operation Barbarossa' (after a German emperor in the Middle Ages). The Germans had 3 million soldiers, 3500 tanks and 2700 planes. Hitler told his men to 'flatten Russia like a hailstorm'.

WHY DID HITLER INVADE RUSSIA?

1. Russia had **raw materials** – especially wheat and oil – which Hitler needed for the war.
2. The Nazis believed that Russia would give the German people *lebensraum* ('living space').
3. Racism: the Nazis believed that the Russians (who were Slavs) were inferior to the German 'Aryan' race.
4. The Russians were **communists** – the opposite of the Nazis, who were **fascists**.
5. Hitler had seen the Russian army do badly in Finland in 1939–40. He also knew that, in the 1930s, Stalin had shot 35,000 army officers (almost half of them) because he thought they were plotting against him. Hitler thought he would easily defeat the Russian army, and this tempted him to attack.
6. The Russian army was badly equipped – Russia only had 1500 tanks that were as modern as the German tanks.

Hitler did not know that this was to be the war which would destroy Germany.

'SCORCHED EARTH'

At first, the Germans won victory after victory. The Russians retreated. As they went, they destroyed everything which could be used by the German army for food or shelter.

The Germans captured lots of land and 3 million men. But Stalin had millions more soldiers to send to fight. Also, he had built 1500 factories far in the east of Russia, and they made more tanks and planes. As fast as the Germans destroyed the Russian army, more men and weapons were sent to keep on fighting.

BATTLES OF ENCIRCLEMENT

Hitler's troops attacked in three prongs. Hitler wanted them to encircle (get round behind) the Russian armies and cut off their retreat.

By the end of 1941, the Army Group North (AGN) had reached Leningrad, the Army Group Centre (AGC) was only 60 km away from Moscow, and the Army Group South (AGS) had conquered the Ukraine. But the Germans had not been able to encircle and destroy the Russian army.

Then winter came. The Germans froze. The Russians counter-attacked. Hitler lost 1 million men. The first year of the war with Russia had ended in a huge setback.

A SOURCE

In 1998 Antony Beevor wrote this about the first day of the invasion.

The German pilots saw hundreds of Russian planes neatly lined up on the runways. In the next nine hours they destroyed 1200 Russian planes, most of them on the ground. Those Russian planes that did get into the air were out-of-date, and no match for the Luftwaffe pilots.

B SOURCE

In 1994 a German pilot remembered an attack on a Russian airfield in 1941.

We dropped the bombs in a line across the field and blew up the runway. No fighters would be able to take off from there for some time. Fifteen Russian planes were in flames. We were so successful that we did not need to make a second attack as we had planned.

C SOURCE

In 1997 the modern historian Richard Overy wrote this about the German invasion.

Stalin had not expected Hitler to invade. Nothing was ready. Planes were lined up in inviting rows. At least 1200 of them were destroyed in the first few hours of the war, most of them on the ground.

D SOURCE

A Soviet poster of 1943 shows a Russian girl in a Nazi prison camp. The words say: 'Our hope is in you, Red Soldier'.

ВСЯ НАДЕЖДА НА ТЕБЯ, КРАСНЫЙ ВОИН

Questions

a What can you learn from Source A about the Soviet Air Force in June 1941?

b Does Source C support the evidence of Sources A and B about the Soviet Air Force in the early days of the invasion?

c How useful are Sources D and E as evidence of German treatment of Soviet civilians?

d 'The German invasion was successful in 1941 because it was well-planned.' Use the sources and your own knowledge to explain whether you agree with this view.

E SOURCE

A photo, published by the Russians in 1942, showing Russian civilians shot by the Nazis.

9 GERMAN DEFEAT IN RUSSIA

Key Issue

- How did the Russians defeat Hitler?

Key Words
- 6th Army • 'not a step back' • Stalingrad
- Zhukov • scorched earth • winter • Citadel
- Kursk • Leningrad • partisans

STALINGRAD: 'NOT A STEP BACK'

Although Operation Barbarossa had been a disaster in 1941, Hitler tried again in 1942. He sent the German Sixth Army to try to capture Stalingrad.

But Stalin now decided that it was time to stop the Germans. 'Not a step back', he told his soldiers. So the Russian soldiers, led by General Zhukov, fought for every room of every house. The Germans captured most of Stalingrad, but they failed to take it all.

Then the Russian winter swept in again, and again the German army froze. The Russians attacked, surrounded and trapped 300,000 Germans. After a brave defence, 90,000 Germans surrendered on 30 January 1943. For Hitler, it was a total defeat.

KURSK: OPERATION CITADEL

After Stalingrad, the Russians began to attack the Germans, to drive them out of Russia.

Hitler did not give up. In July 1943, he tried again to attack and encircle the Russia army at Kursk. He code-named the attack: 'Operation Citadel'. The battle of Kursk was the biggest tank battle in history – the Germans had 2700 tanks and 900,000 men; the Russians, 8200 tanks and more than a million men. The Germans were defeated.

In January 1944, the German siege of Leningrad also failed. The Russians had stopped the Germans, and now they were ready to invade Germany.

WHY DID BARBAROSSA FAIL?

1. Russia was too huge. However many Russian soldiers the Germans killed or captured, more filled their places.
2. Stalin had moved his factories to the east – however many weapons the Germans destroyed, the Russians always sent more.
3. The Russian winter destroyed the German army in 1941 and 1942.
4. Hitler had not planned properly – his men were not given any winter uniforms.
5. The Russian 'scorched earth' policy meant that the Germans had nowhere to shelter.
6. Hitler was overconfident – he thought it would be easy to destroy the Russians, who he thought were an inferior race.
7. The Russians were very brave soldiers – especially at Stalingrad.
8. The Germans were very cruel to the people they conquered, so they were also attacked by **partisans** – civilians who fought behind the lines.

Some historians claim that Russia won the war. Hitler suffered a huge defeat. The British and Americans together defeated 176 divisions of the German army. The Russians destroyed 607 German divisions, and killed 6 million German soldiers.

 SOURCE

In 1965 the historian Alan Clark described the effect of the cold on the Germans.

The German soldiers had no extra clothes except denim overalls, which they pulled over their own clothes and packed with newspaper. There was no shelter – the Russians had destroyed all the buildings, and the ground was too hard to make dug-outs.

B SOURCE

German soldiers captured by the Russians.

C SOURCE

In 1998 the modern historian Antony Beever described how German soldiers tried to cope with the Russian winter.

Many German soldiers were not given winter clothes, so they made their own. They wore Russian uniforms under their own – best of all, a captured Russian quilted jacket!   In the cold, a metal helmet became like a freezer – instead, they wrapped Russian scarves and socks round their heads.

D SOURCE

Russian snipers in their winter uniforms.

E SOURCE

Weapons made in 1941.

	Aircraft	Tanks	Artillery
Russia	15,735	6590	42,300
Germany	11,766	5200	7000

Questions

a What can you learn from Source A about the conditions for German soldiers?
b Does Source C support the evidence of Sources A and B about the effect of the winter on the German troops?
c How useful are Sources D and E as evidence about why the Soviet Union defeated the Germans?
d 'The Germans' biggest mistake was their failure to prepare their troops for the winter cold.'   Use the sources and your own knowledge to explain whether you agree with this view.

Controversy!

'We did not win the war – the Russians did.'
What is your INSTANT REACTION?

10 THE BOMBING OF GERMANY

→ **Key Issue**

• Did bombing Germany help to win the war?

Key Words
• tactical • strategic • revenge • industry
• Stalin • 'Bomber' Harris
• 'thousand bomber raids' • Cologne
• Hamburg • Dresden • anti-aircraft guns

STRATEGIC BOMBING

There are two kinds of bombing:

1. '**Tactical bombing**' – when the bombers are used as part of a battle.
2. '**Strategic bombing**' – when the airforce attacks enemy factories and towns.

At the start of the war, Neville Chamberlain had not allowed the bombing of Germany, but in 1942 Churchill ordered all-out bombing raids on Germany:

1. He wanted revenge for the **Blitz**.
2. He believed that it would destroy Germany's industry.
3. He wanted to destroy the **morale** of the German people.
4. Stalin was complaining that Britain was not doing enough to fight Hitler, and that Russia was having to do all the fighting.

'BOMBER' HARRIS

In February 1942 Arthur 'Bomber' Harris became head of the RAF's Bomber Command. He believed that bombing Germany would win the war and he made 'thousand-bomber raids' on Germany. British bombers attacked at night; American bombers by day:

• In May 1942 a raid on Cologne killed 40,000 people.

• A week-long raid on Hamburg July–August 1943 killed 45,000 people.

• A raid on Dresden in February 1945 killed 35,000 people.

• In all, **Allied** bombing killed 750,000 Germans, many more than the 60,000 British people killed in the Blitz.

Historians disagree whether the raids helped to defeat Germany, or whether they even damaged German industry (see Sources B–F).

The historian Richard Overy has suggested that the raids helped in another way, by forcing the Germans to use guns and planes defending their cities. One third of all the artillery guns made in Germany in 1944 were anti-aircraft guns – guns that would otherwise have been used to fire at the invading Allied soldiers.

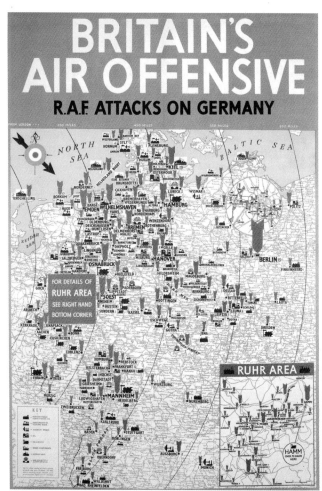

The British poster from 1940 says that British bombing was destroying German industry. Compare this with Source E.

A SOURCE

In 1942 'Bomber' Harris told his bomber crews:

Your main job is to destroy the morale of the German people, especially the factory workers. We will bomb Germany city by city, more and more terribly, until she cannot go on with the war.

B SOURCE

In 1972 the historian Peter Calvocoressi wrote this about the bombing of German cities.

In Berlin the bombing closed the schools, and many people left the city, but most of the factories kept on working. Morale did not break, and the bombing failed to destroy German industry.

C SOURCE

In 1966 Peter Young, a soldier and historian, wrote this about the bombing of Germany.

On 14 October 1943, 291 American bombers attacked the German ball-bearing factories. Sixty planes were shot down, but the factories were damaged, and German industry almost came to a complete stop.

D SOURCE

German industrial output, 1940–4 (coal, steel and oil in millions of tonnes).

	1940	1941	1942	1943	1944
Coal	268	315	318	340	348
Steel	21	28	29	31	26
Oil	5	6	7	8	5
Tanks	2200	5200	9200	17,300	22,100
Aircraft	10,200	11,800	15,400	24,800	39,800

E SOURCE

A photo of Dresden, March 1946.

F SOURCE

In 1995 the modern historian A N Frankland wrote this about the bombing of Germany:

The bombing did not win the war, but it had a very great effect – Germany ran out of oil, its roads and railways were wrecked, and its cities were destroyed. The bombing played a vital part in defeating the Germans.

Questions

a What can you learn from Source A about the RAF's policy of bombing Germany?

b Does Source C support the evidence of Sources A and B about the effect of the Allied bombing of Germany?

c How useful are Sources D and E about the effectiveness of Allied bombing of Germany?

d 'The bombing of Germany had no significant impact on Germany's war effort.' Use the sources and your own knowledge to explain whether you agree with this view.

Controversy!

'Bombing German civilians was wrong. It made us as bad as the Nazis.' **What is your INSTANT REACTION?**

11 D-DAY AND THE DEFEAT OF GERMANY

Key Issue

→ • Why did the D-Day landings succeed?

Key Words
- 'Second Front' • Italy • Stalin • 'Operation Overlord' • 6 June 1944 • Eisenhower • Calais • Kent • Mulberries • Normandy • Romania • Arnhem • Battle of the Bulge • 30 April 1945 • 8 May 1945

THE SECOND FRONT

Stalin wanted Britain and America to open a 'Second Front' by attacking France. He said that this would force the Germans to send soldiers to France, and make it easier for Russia to defeat Germany in eastern Europe. He had been asking for this since 1942.

Stalin expected Britain to invade France in 1943. Instead, Churchill attacked Italy, telling Stalin it would force Hitler to send soldiers to Italy, and make the attack on France easier. This made Stalin angry – he thought that Britain and America were letting Russia do all the fighting, so that Germany and Russia would destroy each other.

'LET'S GO!'

Eventually, the invasion of France – called 'Operation Overlord' – took place on 6 June 1944. General Eisenhower, the American commander of all the **Allied forces**, gave the go-ahead for D-Day with the simple order: 'Let's go!'. (The 'D' in 'D-Day' stands for 'day': it was *the* day – the day that marked the end of Hitler.)

The allies made their attack on the beaches of Normandy. This took the Germans completely by surprise. Even after the first landings, Hitler was sure that Normandy was not the real invasion, and he held back 500 tanks in the Calais area until it was too late – by the time he sent them to Normandy, the Allies were winning the battle.

There were three reasons Hitler thought the attack was not going to be in Normandy:

1. The Allies bombed Calais to make him think they were going to attack there.

2. The Allies set up a mock invasion camp in Kent, with pretend wooden tanks, tents and smokey camp-fires. They kept the real invasion camp (near Portsmouth) very secret, and used smokeless fuel for the fires.

3. Hitler did not think a landing in Normandy was possible, because Normandy has no ports or landing-places.

MULBERRIES

Normandy had no ports, so the Allies had to take their own ports with them. They built floating metal landing ports called **Mulberries**, and towed them across the Channel to France.

On the first day, 60,000 troops fought their way ashore. Within a week there were 300,000 Allied soldiers in France, and after three months there were two million.

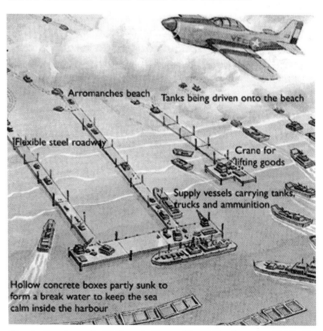

The steel roadway of a Mulberry harbour. The Mulberries were vital for the success of the D-Day landings.

Within the image:
- Arromanches beach
- Tanks being driven onto the beach
- Flexible steel roadway
- Crane for lifting goods
- Supply vessels carrying tanks, trucks and ammunition
- Hollow concrete boxes partly sunk to form a break water to keep the sea calm inside the harbour

The Germans were not strong enough to stop them. Hitler had 600,000 soldiers. The German airforce in northern France was weak (see Source A), and in August 1944 Romania joined the Allies – so Hitler lost a quarter of his oil supplies.

THE INVASION OF GERMANY

After the success of the Normandy landings, the Allies were able to advance into Germany. They had just two setbacks:

ARNHEM

The British used lightly-armed paratroopers to take some bridges in Holland, which they hoped the advancing army would use. But Arnhem was 'a bridge too far', and the Germans were able to defeat the paratroopers before the main army broke through to them. Of the 10,000 men who made the attack, 8,000 died.

THE BATTLE OF THE BULGE

In December 1944, Hitler made a last attack to try to stop the Allies invading Germany. At first, the Germans were successful, but by January 1945 they had been stopped, and the Allies invaded Germany.

HITLER IS DEFEATED

Hitler had used his last forces in the Battle of the Bulge. In April 1945, the Russians captured Berlin, and Hitler shot himself (30 April 1945). Germany surrendered on 8 May 1945. Hitler had said that his empire would 'last a thousand years'. He had managed 12.

B SOURCE

German defences at Calais in Northern France, 1944.

C SOURCE

In 1966 Peter Young, a soldier and a historian, described how the German defenders were fooled in 1944.

The bombing of Calais was very heavy. The Germans never realised the attack would be in Normandy.

D SOURCE

In 1995 the modern historian Richard Overy wrote this about the Normandy invasion.

Hitler knew how important the D-Day landings were. If he had defeated the Allied invasion, he could have gone on to win the war.

Questions

a According to Source A, why were the Allies able to control the skies on D-Day?

b How useful is Source B to an historian studying the Allied invasion of Normandy in June 1944? Use Source B and your own knowledge to answer this question.

c Using Source C and your own knowledge, explain why the Germans were convinced the Allied invasion would be in the Calais area.

d 'An Allied defeat in June 1944 would have led to a German victory in the war.' Is this a fair interpretation? Use Source D and your own knowledge to answer this question.

A SOURCE

In 1995 the modern historian Richard Overy wrote this about the German airforce on D-Day.

The German airforce did little in the battle. On June 6th, against 12,000 Allied planes, the Germans could send only 170 planes. Most of the planes were destroyed as the Allied planes attacked the airfields in northern France. Many German pilots were not fully trained, and some got lost. They were easily shot out of the skies.

Key Issue

• What was the main reason for Germany's defeat?

Key Words

- industrial strength • Russia • America
- Christian democracy • Italy • Barbarossa
- atrocities • resistance groups
- strategic bombing • 'control of the skies'

WAS GERMANY DOOMED TO LOSE THE WAR?

At first, it seems obvious why Germany was defeated in the Second World War. If you look at Source C, you will see that the **Allies** were so much stronger industrially that they could produce more weapons and keep going longer than the Germans.

Some historians have suggested that Germany was doomed to lose the war – especially when the USA joined in.

But is that all there is to it? The historian Neil de Marco does not think so. He wrote (1997):

Overwhelming industrial power doesn't always lead to victory in war. The United States found this out 30 years later when it lost the Vietnam War. It is not enough to have more of everything.

Historians have suggested other reasons that Germany lost the war. Read the suggestions on pages 27–28, then debate as a class which factor you think was the main reason for Germany's defeat.

*At first, some people supported the Germans because they feared **communism**. This poster invites Belgians to join the German army to fight the Russians. But, as the war went on, more and more people saw the German conquerors as the real enemy.*

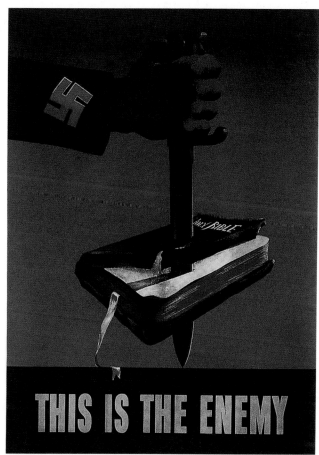

*Many Britains and Americans believed they were fighting to save Christian **democracy** from a new dark age. This gave them the moral will to win.*

RUSSIA

In the year before Stalingrad, Germany produced four times as much steel as Russia, but the Germans were still defeated. Why?

1. Stalin moved his factories away from the war zone to the east, where they could produce weapons without being attacked.
2. The Russian 'scorched earth' policy stopped the Germans taking over Russian factories or farms.
3. The German factories insisted on producing a range of models to a very high quality. The Russians churned out thousands of the same thing. In 1943, for example, the Russians produced 8m tons of steel, but made 48,000 artillery guns; the Germans produced 30m tons of steel, but made only 24,000 big guns. The Germans had 42 kinds of plane; the Russians just five.
4. The Russians were fighting to free their land from the invader; the German soldiers hated being sent to the **Eastern front**.

AMERICA

America produced more steel, oil and cars than the rest of the world put together. What was amazing about the American war effort was that America managed so quickly to turn its production around and to start making weapons.

1. Henry Kaiser invented a way of building ships – called '**Liberty** ships' – using **pre-fabricated** parts. Where before it had taken a year to build a ship, a Liberty ship could be built in 41 days.
2. The car industry stopped making cars for ordinary people. Instead, the car factories made jeeps and troop carriers.
3. Henry Ford – who had invented the assembly line – found a way to mass-produce B-24 **Liberator** planes. Ford's factory made one B-24 every hour.

ITALY

Hitler's alliance with Italy was a disaster for Germany. Italy invaded North Africa in 1940 – and did so badly that Germany had to send an army to help. Then, in 1943, Italy surrendered, leaving the German army alone to fight the Allied forces advancing through Italy.

Hitler blamed the Italians for losing him the war.

'BARBAROSSA' – THE BIGGEST MISTAKE

It could be easily argued that Hitler's invasion of Russia was the turning point. The Russians destroyed three times as many German divisions as Britain and America, and it was the Russians who captured Berlin in April 1945.

GERMAN ATROCITIES

The Nazis were cruel conquerors. They killed Jews and punished any opposition. **Resistance** groups were set up in France, Poland and Russia. They bombed railways, helped Allied soldiers to escape, and passed on vital information to the Allies.

AIRCRAFT: THE KEY TO VICTORY

Some historians argue that it was not just general industrial power that helped the Allies win the war, but production of one thing: the plane. The Allies could build planes much faster than the Germans. This helped them win the war for two reasons:

1. **Strategic bombing** raids damaged German factories, and used up Hitler's forces defending German cities against the bombers. In 1944 one-third of all the artillery guns made in Germany, and two-thirds of all the planes, were used to try to stop the Allied bombing raids.
2. **Tactical bombing** was vital in the D-Day landings. In June 1944, Hitler had enough troops in northern France to defeat the Allied invasion. But he only had 170 planes, whereas the Allies had 12,000 planes, and the Allies' control of the skies meant that they were successful.

Industrial power, Russia, America, Italy, Barbarossa, atrocities or air power? What the most important reason was for Germany's defeat is a matter of argument, and you may wish to debate this as a class before you attempt the questions on page 29.

A SOURCE

A German soldier said this after the Normandy landings of 1944.

I cannot understand these Americans. Each night we know that we have cut them to pieces, killed them, destroyed their trucks. Yet each morning we are faced with fresh troops, new trucks and weapons. This happens every day.

B SOURCE

This 1944 German poster reads: 'Just as we fight — so will you work for victory!'

SOURCE

German and Allied production in 1944.

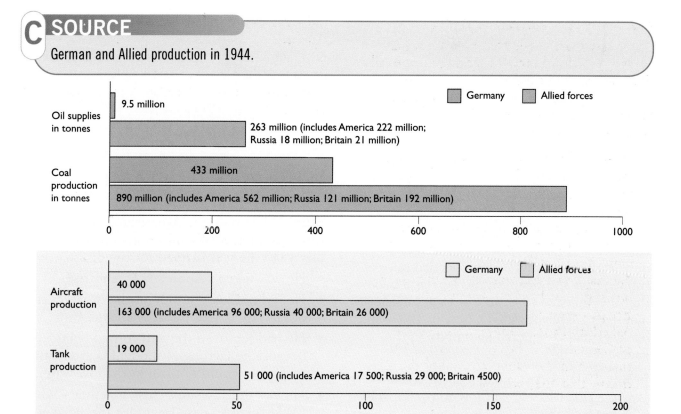

SOURCE D

In 1995 the modern historian Richard Overy wrote this about why the Allies won.

The key to the Allied victory was the army and industry of Russia, which first stopped, and then defeated, the Germans.

Make brief notes on why Germany lost the war under these headings:
- Industrial output • Russia • America
  • Italy • Barbarossa • atrocities
    • aircraft

Write a conclusion linking these ideas together.

Questions

a What does Source A tell us about US military power at the time of the Normandy landings?

b Why was Source B distributed in Germany in 1944? Use Source B and your own knowledge to answer this question.

c How useful is Source C to an historian studying the reasons for Germany's defeat? Use Source C and your own knowledge to answer this question.

d Is Source D an accurate interpretation of why Germany lost the war? Use Source D and your own knowledge to answer this question.

Controversy!

'It would be nice to think that the war was won by individual heroism, community spirit and the British national character.

But the sad truth is that the war was won by boring statistics – how many tons of steel, how many bullets, how many planes.'

What is your INSTANT REACTION?

13 THE WAR IN THE PACIFIC

Key Issue

• Why were the Americans taken by surprise?

Key Words
• Japan • oil • 1937: China • July 1941
• Pearl Harbor: 'a day of infamy'
• aircraft carriers • Kimmel • Roosevelt

There were two great powers in the Pacific – America and Japan. America was more powerful industrially. Japan needed oil, rubber, iron and rice, and the Japanese believed that they needed to go to war to get these **raw materials**. They invaded China in 1937, and by 1941 had conquered an empire in the Pacific.

In July 1941, America banned the sale of oil to Japan. This was a great blow to the Japanese, who got two-thirds of their oil from America.

The Japanese government decided that it would have to go to war with America. But the Japanese would only have a chance of winning a war against America if they struck first. So they decided on a surprise attack on the American naval base at Pearl Harbor, in Hawaii.

PEARL HARBOR

The Japanese fleet sailed across the Pacific to within 450 km of Hawaii. On 7 December 1941, two waves of Japanese planes attacked the 70 ships in Pearl Harbor. They sank six American battleships plus ten other ships, destroyed 164 planes, and killed 2400 people.

The attack did not destroy the American fleet. Most importantly, the three American aircraft carriers were not in port.

What the attack did do, however, was make all Americans very angry – President Roosevelt declared it 'a day of **infamy**', and ordered the war which would end in Hiroshima and the defeat of Japan four years later.

WHO WAS TO BLAME?

Admiral Kimmel, the American commander, was found guilty of neglect and sacked. For fifty years, he was blamed for the disaster.

• He was taken completely by surprise.

• He did not keep watch on the ocean north of Hawaii, where the attack came from.

• He had removed the anti-torpedo nets because he (wrongly) thought that Japanese torpedoes could not run in shallow water.

• He had put the ships close together – which made them an easy target for the Japanese planes.

• He had given his men time off the night before the attack.

Recently, however, historians have found records which seem to show that Roosevelt and the American government:

• Knew Japan was going to declare war.

• Knew where the Japanese fleet was.

• Knew there was going to be an attack (and perhaps even knew it was going to be at Pearl Harbor).

• Decided, on purpose, not to tell Kimmel.

A SOURCE

In 1982 the historian John Toland claimed that the Americans knew – from a message decoded on 6 December 1941– that the Japanese were planning to go to war.

President Roosevelt read it and said: 'This means war'. But the message was not sent to the fleet's commander, Admiral Kimmel. In fact, no decoded Japanese messages had been sent to Admiral Kimmel for months. Some people wanted to tell him, but they were not allowed to do so.

B SOURCE

Map of the Pacific Ocean in 1941.

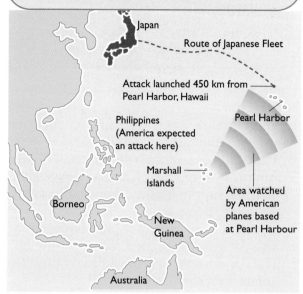

Japan
Route of Japanese Fleet
Attack launched 450 km from Pearl Harbor, Hawaii
Pearl Harbor
Philippines (America expected an attack here)
Marshall Islands
Area watched by American planes based at Pearl Harbour
Borneo
New Guinea
Australia

C SOURCE

In 1995 the historian I C B Dear wrote this about the attack on Pearl Harbor.

Admiral Kimmel did not know where the Japanese fleet was. He had been told to watch the Japanese Marshall Islands (south of Pearl Harbor), and three long-range reconnaissance planes were on patrol there. But the Japanese came from the north.

D SOURCE

A photo of a burning American ship, 1941.

E SOURCE

An American poster, 1942.

AVENGE December 7

F SOURCE

In 1979 the historian William Manchester wrote this about the attack on Pearl Harbor.

American commanders were told to expect a Japanese attack 'in the next few days'. Admiral Kimmel decided to ignore this. On December 6, he gave his men the evening off. Only 195 of the 780 anti-aircraft guns were manned, and most of them had no ammunition – it had been sent back to storage 'to stop it getting dusty'.

Questions

a What can you learn from Source A about the Japanese attack on Pearl Harbor in December 1941?

b Does Source C support the evidence of Sources A and B about the attack on Pearl Harbor?

c How useful are Sources D and E as evidence about the effects of the attack on Pearl Harbor?

d 'Admiral Kimmel was to blame for the disaster at Pearl Harbor.' Use the sources and your own knowledge to explain whether you agree with this view.

14 THE DEFEAT OF JAPAN

Key Issue

- Why did the Japanese lose the war?

Key Words

- 'sneak attack' • 'island-hopping'
- atomic bomb • Okinawa • rice

JAPAN'S GAMBLE

Japan's leaders knew that they did not have the industrial power to defeat America in a war. Japan **imported** 80% of its iron and oil, and did not have any copper or rubber at all. It had to import 2 million tonnes of rice a year to feed its people.

The Japanese plan was to destroy the American navy in the surprise attack on Pearl Harbor, and then – before the Americans recovered – to conquer so huge an empire that the Americans would not dare go to war. When the attack on Pearl Harbor did not destroy the American navy, the Japanese plan failed.

What was worse, the 'sneak' attack made the Americans angry, and determined to defeat Japan.

There were five more reasons that the Japanese lost the war:

1. Their empire was spread all over the Pacific, and was difficult to defend.
2. They did not use their submarines to attack American shipping. (Instead they used them to supply food to their soldiers on the different islands.)
3. The American plan of 'island-hopping'.
4. The Americans stopped Japan getting oil.
5. The Americans used the atomic bomb (for points 3–5, see Chapter 15).

SHORTAGES

At first, the Japanese government tried to keep secret the news of defeats like the battle of Midway. As time went on, however, the Japanese people realised that they were losing the war:

1. The Americans captured the island of Okinawa, and began to bomb Japan.
2. There were food shortages because American submarines sank 85% of Japan's **merchant ships** – in 1944 Japan was able to import only a third of the rice it needed.

A SOURCE

Production of raw materials in Japan and America in 1937:

	Coal	Oil	Iron	Copper	Wheat
America	Exports	Exports	Enough	Exports	Enough
Japan	Not enough	None	Not enough	None	Not enough

Note:
- 'exports' means that the country had enough for its own needs and was able to sell the rest to other countries;
- 'enough' means that the country had enough for its own needs;
- 'not enough' means that the country did not have enough for its own needs;
- 'none' means that the country had no supplies of this raw material.

B SOURCE

What different raw materials were used for:

	USES
Coal	fuel for power stations; making iron and steel; explosives.
Oil	fuel for tanks, trucks, ships and planes
Iron ore	making the steel needed for tanks, ships, planes, shells, weapons etc.
Copper	electric wires; also used to make bullets and shells
Wheat	bread

C SOURCE

Japanese and American production, 1944.

	Japan	America
Aircraft	28,000	96,000
Machine-guns	380,000	2,700,000
Aircraft carriers	5	45

D SOURCE

An American poster, 1944.

...we here highly resolve that these dead shall not have died in vain...

REMEMBER DEC. 7th!

E SOURCE

The effects of American bombing on Japanese cities, March–May 1945.

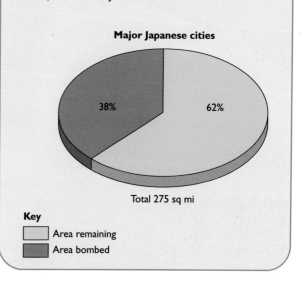

Major Japanese cities

38%   62%

Total 275 sq mi

Key
- Area remaining
- Area bombed

F SOURCE

In 1988 the historian Paul Kennedy wrote this about how Japanese troops were spread out in 1945.

Even when Japan was on the verge of defeat in 1945, there were 1 million Japanese soldiers in China, and another 780,000 in Manchuria, and these could not be moved to help defend Japan.

Questions

a What can you learn from Source A about why Japan was defeated in the war?

b Does Source C support the evidence of Sources A and B about why Japan was defeated?

c How useful are Sources D and E as evidence of why Japan was defeated?

d 'Japan was defeated because it could not produce enough weapons.' Use the sources and your own knowledge to explain whether you agree with this view.

Make brief notes on the defeat of Japan under the following headings:
- Six reasons Japan lost the war
- How the war affected the Japanese people

15 AMERICAN VICTORY

Key Issue

- Did the Americans need to drop the atomic bomb to make Japan surrender?

For a while after Pearl Harbor, Japan did very well in the war. In February 1942, the Japanese captured Singapore, capturing 62,000 British prisoners-of-war.

However, in June 1942, the American navy defeated the Japanese at the battle of Midway. Four Japanese aircraft carriers were destroyed. This was a great blow to the Japanese because they only managed to build another seven aircraft carriers in the next two years – the Americans built 90. Slowly, the Americans, British and Australians drove back the Japanese.

ISLAND HOPPING

Two things helped the **Allies** defeat Japan:

1. *'Island-hopping'*. The Americans did not try to recapture every island held by the Japanese. Instead, they leap-frogged over unimportant ones and well-defended ones, cutting them off from their supplies.
2. *The Americans stopped Japan getting oil*. The Americans conquered the Philippines in 1944, cutting off Japan from 80% of its supplies of oil.

The Japanese soldiers were brave and fanatical. They believed they had to fight to the death. When the Americans captured Iwo Jima, a tiny island, in 1945, 22,000 of the 23,000 Japanese soldiers fought to the death. Nearly 6,000 American soldiers were killed, and the battle took more than a month.

In June 1945, the Americans captured the island of Okinawa. The Americans lost 13,000 men and the battle took two months of fierce fighting. But, from Okinawa, American planes could bomb Japan.

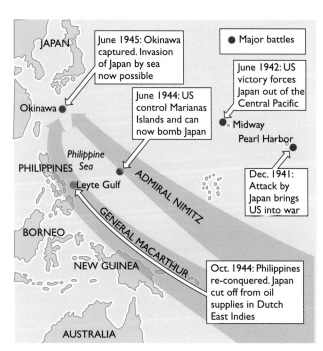

The American plan to conquer Japan used land forces under General MacArthur and the navy under Admiral Nimitz.

THE ATOMIC BOMB

The American government was worried how many American soldiers would die if they tried to capture Japan itself.

On 6 August 1945, the Americans dropped an atomic bomb on Hiroshima in Japan. On 9 August 1945 they dropped a second atomic bomb on Nagasaki. On 10 August 1945, the Japanese surrendered. There were many people who said that the atomic bomb was evil, and that the Americans should not have used it. But, at the time, it was felt that the atomic bomb brought the war to an end, and saved the lives of thousands of American soldiers who would otherwise have had to invade Japan.

Recently, however, historians have questioned whether the atomic bomb was really needed. The Japanese did not care about civilian deaths – they had ignored the deaths of 85,000 people when the Americans fire-bombed Tokyo in March 1945. Some modern historians suggest that Japan surrendered because President Truman of America changed his mind and agreed to let the Japanese Emperor Hirohito stay on the throne.

A SOURCE

In 1993 two modern American historians wrote this about the effects of the atomic bomb.

No one knows how long the fanatical Japanese army would have gone on fighting. It is clear that the atomic bomb (and the fact that Russia declared war on Japan) forced the Japanese government to surrender.

B SOURCE

In 1995 the modern British historian Richard Overy wrote this about the atomic bomb.

The Atomic bomb did not win the war, because Japan was already beaten and about to surrender when it was dropped. Tanks, planes, artillery and submarines won the war.

C SOURCE

In 1996 the modern historian Nigel Smith wrote this in a school textbook.

Some Americans said the bomb should be exploded somewhere safe, to warn the Japanese what was coming. Historians today think Japan was about to surrender anyway.

D SOURCE

The *Evening News* newspaper, 8 August 1945.

E SOURCE

Photo of Hiroshima, taken September 1945.

F SOURCE

In 1975 the historian Philip Knightley wrote this about the defeat of Japan.

What defeated Japan was stopping her vital supplies of oil. In 1942, Japan got almost half her oil from her empire; in 1945, none. With or without the atomic bomb, Japan was finished – her ships, planes, tanks and trucks could not move. They had no fuel.

Questions

a What can you learn from Source A about why Japan surrendered in 1945?

b Does Source C support the evidence of Sources A and B about why Japan surrendered in 1945?

c How useful are Sources D and E as evidence about the effect of the atomic bombing of Hiroshima?

d 'The use of the atomic bombs against Japan was unnecessary.' Use the sources and your own knowledge to explain whether you agree with this view.

Key Words

- February 1942: Singapore • June 1942: Midway • aircraft carriers • 'island-hopping' • oil • fanatical • Iwo Jima • Okinawa • March 1945: firebombing of Tokyo • Truman • 6 August 1945: Hiroshima • 9 August: Nagasaki • Emperor Hirohito

Key Issue

- How did the government use propaganda and censorship during the war?

Key Words

- conscription • ARP • Buckingham Palace • morale • Mass Observation • MoI • propaganda • humour • Fifth Columnists • internment • 'Category C' • 'Category A' • Italians: 'collar the lot' • BBC • truth • *ITMA* • *Music While You Work* • Vera Lynn • censorship • 'black propaganda' • PWE

This is where we came in;
This has happened before
Only last time there was cheering.

This poem shows how the British people went to war. There was no cheering like in 1914. They were ready for war, not happy for war.

In 1939, Britain had brought in **conscription**, and 100,000 people had joined the ARP (air raid precautions) as air-raid wardens. But most people did not want to go war. They were business-like about the whole thing – it was something that had to be done.

In September 1940 a German bomb hit Buckingham Palace. Churchill gave the attack a lot of publicity – he knew it would make the British people angry, and unite them behind the King and Queen.

MASS OBSERVATION

> **Propaganda** is where a government publishes things to make people think what it wants them to think.

The government worried about the **morale** of the British people. In 1937 it had set up a unit called 'Mass Observation' to find out what people thought.

Mass Observation talked to ordinary people, and reported what people were saying in pubs and shops. Sometimes they reported that the government was failing, for example after Dunkirk they reported that public morale was very low. Government propaganda was written by upper class, university people who did not understand how ordinary people thought or felt.

The Ministry of Information (MoI) was set up in 1939 to keep the public informed about the war, and to keep up public morale. From the start it decided not to try to cover up British defeats, or exaggerate British victories. This was very brave, because the news was almost all bad until 1942. Some historians think that the MoI did not do a very good job.

FIFTH COLUMNISTS

British propaganda was best when it was funny, and laughed at Hitler and the Germans. Source B is an example from a set of posters trying to stop people giving away information to German spies.

The government was worried that **Fifth Columnists** (British people who wanted Germany to win the war) would undermine the war effort. At first it asked people to tell the police about people who made defeatist comments. But nobody liked doing this – it made them feel like the Nazis they were fighting to defeat. It was stopped after some silly incidents (such as the Scots woman who was arrested on a visit to London because no one could understand her accent).

INTERNMENT

The government was also worried about Germans who lived in Britain. By the end of November 1939, 74,000 Germans had been interviewed to see if they were loyal.

64,000 were said to be 'Category C' – loyal (some of them were Jews, or people who had left Germany because they hated the Nazis).

At first only 600 Germans were **interned** (imprisoned) because they were 'Category A' – a danger to Britain. During 1940, when it seemed that Hitler was going to invade, this number grew, and women were also interned.

When Italy declared war on Britain in 1940, Churchill ordered all Italians in Britain to be arrested. 'Collar the lot!', he said, and by July 1940, 27,000 Germans and Italians had been interned. By the summer of 1941, when the fear of invasion had fallen, this number had fallen to 5,000.

This German poster shows how much radio broadcasts worried the Germans – it calls Germans who listened to them Verrater *('traitors'). Can you see the word* Soldatensender *('soldier-radio': the Germans' name for the PWE)?*

THE BBC

The great thing about British propaganda was the BBC. The BBC was not under government control, but it was very careful to follow MoI guidelines. People all over the world – both enemies and allies – trusted the BBC to tell the truth. So that the Germans could not fool people by pretending to be the BBC, newsreaders always started by telling listeners their name, so people would be able to spot a fake broadcast.

The BBC kept up morale by popular programmes such as the comedy *ITMA* ('It's That Man Again') and *Sincerely Yours* (a programme in which Vera Lynn sang songs for British soldiers). Eight million war-workers listened to *Music While You Work*, a programme to improve production in British factories.

> **Censorship** is where a government stops you knowing things it does not want you to know.

CENSORSHIP

Newspapers were not allowed to show photos of people killed by enemy bombing. The press and radio were not allowed to say anything which would give away army movements. Also, letters written home by soldiers were read by their officers, and anything that might help the enemy was crossed out with a thick blue pencil line.

In general, censorship in Britian was mild.

A SOURCE

In 1986 the historian Peter Lewis wrote this about how the Ministry of Information publicised the bombing of Buckingham Palace in 1940.

The Ministry of Information tried to cover up the bombing. 'Idiots! Fools!' said Churchill when he heard this. 'Tell everyone! Let the people of London know that the King and Queen are in danger from the bombs – just like they are,' he said.

BLACK PROPAGANDA

In 1941 the government set up a department called the Political Warfare Executive. It used '**black propaganda**' (lies) to trick the Germans.

The PWE set up a radio station which pretended to be broadcast by a group of German soldiers who hated Hitler. Most of the information broadcast by the PWE was the turth, but it attacked the British and said that Churchill was 'a flat-footed bastard of a drunken old Jew' – so people believed the reports were genuine. From time to time, the PWE would put in a trick report to confuse and upset the Germans.

On one occasion, the PWE published a list of German cities bombed by the RAF, but added that any German soldier who lived there could get a pass to visit his family. When the soldiers tried to get the pass, not only were they told they could not have one (which upset them) but they got into trouble for listening to foreign radio.

B SOURCE

A famous propaganda poster.

You never know who's listening!

CARELESS TALK COSTS LIVES

This photo from January 1943, shows children killed by a bomb which fell on a school. No one ever saw the photo – the censors banned it.

In 1989 the historian John Campbell wrote this about the effect of the BBC.

The BBC was powerful propaganda because people believed it. It did not try to cover up British defeats, and it did not exaggerate British victories.

Make brief notes under the following headings:
- Mass Observation
- Fith Columnists and Internment
- Role of the BBC
- Censorship
- Black propaganda

Questions

a According to Source A, why was Churchill so angry with the Ministry of Information?

b Why was Source C censored by the government? Use Source C and your own knowledge to answer this question.

c How useful is Source B to an historian studying Britain during the war? Use Source B and your own knowledge to answer this question.

d Is Source D an accurate interpretation of the importance of the BBC during the war? Use Source D and your own knowledge to answer this question.

17 THE BLITZ

Key Issue

- What was life like during the Blitz?

Key Words
- Berlin • 76 nights
- Liverpool, Birmingham, Coventry • ports
- searchlights • Underground • LDV ('Home Guard' or 'Dad's Army') • Baedecker raids
- V-1 ('doodlebug') • V-2

At the beginning of the war, both sides did not bomb civilian targets. But then, in August 1940, the RAF bombed Berlin, and an angry Hitler ordered the first bombing raid on London (on 7 September 1940). The German bombers came almost every night for 76 nights. Londoners called this 'the **Blitz**'.

At first, London was the only target but, later, the Germans bombed other British cities, such as Liverpool, Birmingham and Coventry (which had many aircraft factories). After February 1941, they bombed British ports such as Plymouth, Swansea, Belfast and Portsmouth.

There was little the British could do against the Blitz in 1940. Searchlights could only see to 3600 metres (so the Germans just flew higher than this) and RAF night-fighters were not very successful (in one 400-bomber raid on 15 October 1940, the RAF shot down just one German plane). The Blitz did not defeat the British people, but many Londoners went to sleep in the Underground, and the Blitz had a bad effect on **morale** in some places.

THE HOME GUARD

Faced with the threat of invasion, the government set up the LDV (local defence volunteers) in May 1940. By June 1940, 1.5 million men had joined. They watched out for German attacks, and did things like putting old buses in fields to stop German gliders landing there.

Churchill renamed the LDV 'the Home Guard', but most people called them 'Dad's Army'. They were a bit of a laughing stock. They were all either too young or too old to join the army, and at first they had no guns – they used broomsticks instead.

THE BAEDEKER RAIDS

There was a lull in bombing raids after May 1941, until April 1942, when the Germans bombed historic towns like York and Bath in revenge for some RAF raids on historic German cities the month before. These raids were called 'Baedeker raids' after a famous German guide book about Britain. The raids made the Nazis seem like stupid vandals.

THE SECOND BLITZ

By 1944, the RAF controlled the skies, so there were no more German bombing raids. Instead, however, Hitler launched two new '**vengeance** weapons' against the British:

1. The V-1 ('**doodlebug**') was a flying bomb which fell to earth when it ran out of petrol. The buzz of its engine frightened British people, who never knew where it was going to land. Hitler launched 10,000 doodlebugs in the last year of the war, and – though only 3500 of them landed in built-up areas – they killed 6200 people.
2. The V-2 rocket-bombs carried a 1 ton bomb and flew at 4000 kilometres per hour. From September 1944–March 1945, 5000 V-2s were fired by the Germans, killing nearly 3000 British civilians.

The V-weapons did not win the war but, after the war, captured V-2 design papers were used to start the American space programme.

SOURCE

In 1986 a London woman remembered what it was like to sleep in the Underground.

It you were late you had to sit up all night with nothing to lean on because there was no room. Most people managed to lie down, but few got more than 2 or 3 hours sleep. You had to leave a yard on the platform for people to get off the trains.

D SOURCE

A government report about Portsmouth during the Blitz.

People are stealing from bombed shops and the police cannot stop them. There is no community spirit. Morale is bad and people are saying that it is hopeless, and that nothing can be done.

B SOURCE

Londoners asleep in an underground station (1940).

Questions

a According to Source A, what was it like sleeping in an underground station?

b Look at Source B. Why were so many Londoners using underground stations to sleep in at night in 1940? Use Source B and your own knowledge to answer this question.

c How useful is Source C to an historian studying the effect of the Blitz on the civilian population? Use Source C and your own knowledge to answer this question.

d Is Source D an accurate interpretation of the state of civilian morale in Britain during the Blitz? Use Source D and your own knowledge to answer this question.

C SOURCE

A photo of a London family next to the ruins of their bombed Anderson shelter.

<u>18</u> CIVILIAN MORALE

Key Issue

- Did morale hold up during the Blitz?

The Blitz was the time when the war started for most British people.

RESULTS OF THE BLITZ

1. The *Luftwaffe* lost very few planes during the **Blitz** – only about 3 planes from every 200 sent. (This compares very well with the RAF's record against Germany – about 15 planes lost out of every 200 sent).
2. 40,000 British people were killed and 2 million were made homeless.
3. The Americans felt sadness and respect for the Londoners during the Blitz, and they sent money and weapons to help Britain.
4. The Blitz did not break the **morale** of the British people. If anything, it made them more determined to defeat the Germans
5. The shared danger of the Blitz brought the people of London closer together.
6. The failure of the Blitz damaged the morale of the Germans, who had expected to conquer Britain easily. In the end, they decided that the British must be so tough because they were a 'Germanic' people (though not as good as the Germans).

HOW DID PEOPLE COPE?

Britain's anti-aircraft guns and night-fighters were not very successful, but the government did bring in defences such as barrage balloons (to make the bombers fly higher). Also, all lights had to be turned off (the 'blackout') so the German bombers could not see where to drop their bombs. These, however, made things more dangerous for civilians, because they made the German bombing less accurate.

TAKING SHELTER

The government tried to protect civilians:

1. In 1939, the government gave out 38 million gas masks. In the end, the Germans did not use poison gas attacks, but many people carried their gas masks with them just in case. Even babies' prams were made gas-proof.
2. The government gave out 2 million 'Anderson shelters' in cities likely to be bombed (they were given free to poor families). Anderson shelters were made of corrugated iron, and people put them in a hole they dug at the bottom of their garden. People did not like them because they were cold and damp, and they did not protect people from a direct hit.
3. The government built brick public shelters, but people hated them. They were crowded and smelly, and not safe from a direct hit.
4. At first, the government forbade people to use the Underground stations for shelter (they thought it would look as though morale was bad). However, after October 1940, the government was forced to let people go there for shelter. The deepest stations were very popular, and people began to queue for a place on the platform from as early as 10 o'clock in the morning. People were so desperate to get a sleeping place that sometimes fights broke out.
5. Sleeping in the Underground was a terrible thing – it was uncomfortable and there were no toilets. When he was made Home Secretary in October 1940, Herbert Morrison put 200,000 bunks and proper toilets into the Underground stations. He also ordered tube trains with food and drink to stop at Underground stations last thing at night and first thing in the morning.
6. Morrison also ordered very safe, deep shelters for 70,000 people to be dug.
7. Morrison also gave out steel-framed 'Morrison shelters' which people could use in their own home. People liked the Morrison shelters best of all, because they could stay in their own home.

'LAST ORDERS'?

In the end, nowhere was totally safe from a direct hit, and some people decided to stay in the pubs, drinking and singing as loud as they could to drown out the sound of the bombs.

In the towns outside London, many people 'trekked' out into the countryside each night to get away from the bombs. They slept in barns, sheds, and even under hedges. The government did not like this, because it gave the impression that morale was bad.

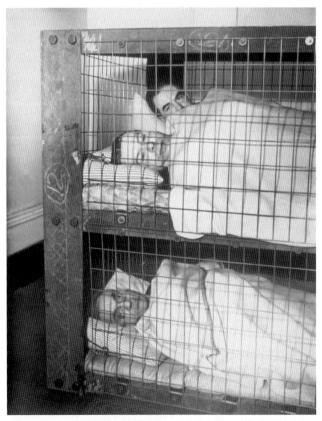

A Morrison shelter from the 1942 government catalogue. They were free to poor people and could be used as a table.

CLEANING UP

Before the war, the government had got a million coffins ready for the people who it expected to be killed. In the end, many fewer people died – it was the large number of survivors that surprised the government. At first, people whose houses had been bombed had to be crammed into local halls, with only a few buckets serving as toilets for hundreds of people. (Later, the government gave them the houses of people who had left London, and it also built temporary houses.)

Another problem that took the government by surprise was **looting**. A looter could be put to death, though this was never used. However, especially in poor areas, many people did rob bombed houses and shops, and rescue workers and firemen often stole things they found in bombed-out houses. Some of them saw it as a reward for the horrible job they were doing.

RESCUE WORK

The Germans used different kinds of bombs which caused different kinds of damage:

- HEs (high explosives) simply blew a huge crater in the ground.
- **Incendiaries** caused fires.
- Parachute bombs fell more slowly and exploded above the ground, which caused more damage.
- Delayed-action bombs went off after they had dropped – they caused a lot of trouble, because the whole area had to be cleared until they were defused.

Building workers were the best rescue workers, because they understood how the buildings had been built. Sometimes the dead showed no signs of injury – the blast alone had killed them. But sometimes the bombs caused terrible wounds, and recovering a blown-up body was a terrible job. Broken gas pipes and unexploded bombs made rescue work even more difficult and dangerous. Yet rescue workers were paid only £3 a week – less than most other workers.

Temporary homes, outside London, built for people whose homes had been bombed.

DID MORALE HOLD UP?

The government was very afraid of defeatism, and Mass Observation did report examples of bad morale:

1. In some places people blamed the Jews for the bombing. They said the Jews were 'grabbing the best shelters'. Some people even said that the Jews in Germany had 'got what they deserved'.
2. In some places there was looting of bombed shops and houses, which the government saw as a very bad sign.
3. The King and Queen were booed when they visited the East End, and Churchill was booed by a crowd of East Enders in 1944.
4. Many poor people in the East End became very angry. As they lived close to the docks, they were bombed much more than the rich people who lived on the outskirts of London. They were in great danger, while the rich people in posh West End hotels had fewer bombs and safer, posher shelters. On one occasion poor people took over the bomb shelter at the Savoy hotel as a protest.

In spite of all this, the Blitz did not break the people's spirit. Towards the end of the war, a new kind of spirit took over, as people began to think about the kind of Britain they wanted after the war (see Chapter 24).

(see Chapter 24)

A SOURCE

Harold Nicolson, a well-known politician of the time, wrote this (17 September 1940) in his diary.

The people of the East End are very angry. It is said that even the King and Queen were booed the other day when they went to see the destroyed areas, and some people fear there will be a revolution.

A government photo to show how good the public brick-built shelters were.

In 1996 the modern historian Philip Ziegler wrote this about London during the Blitz.

Many poor people were angry at the rich. Rich people put deep concrete cellars and luxury bomb shelters into their houses – one cost £180 [£7000 in today's money] and had a toilet and two bedrooms. Rich people escaped to the countryside in their cars to get away from the bombs – and drove past the poor people who had to walk.

Questions

a What does Source A tell you about how people reacted to the Blitz?
b Look at Source B. Why did the government produce this photograph in late 1940? Use Source B and your own knowledge to answer this question.
c How useful is Source C to an historian studying Britain during the Blitz? Use Source C and your own knowledge to answer this question.
d Is Source D an accurate interpretation of wartime spirit in England during the Blitz? Use Source D and your own knowledge to answer this question.

A British wartime poster showing an anti-aircraft gun.

Controversy!

'They survived the Blitz, with its bombs, fire and destruction, and its discomforts, hardships and tiredness. They won the war. Churchill said that the Blitz showed: "the spirit of the British nation, and the tough fibre of the Londoners".
  They were human beings of a higher calibre than us. If Hitler were to Blitz us today, we would capitulate within a week.'
  What is your INSTANT REACTION?

19 EVACUATION

Key Issue

What were the effects of evacuation?

Key Words

• evacuation • homesick • farm animals
• problem children • shocking • Welfare State

Even before the war, the government knew that London would be bombed. It thought that the sight of dead children would be bad for **morale** so, even before the war, it made plans to **evacuate** children from London.

It was a huge task. As soon as war broke out, 800,000 schoolchildren, and 520,000 mothers and children under 5, were sent to live in the country.

Some people could not bear to see their children leave, and refused to send them, but not many. Others brought their children home during the **phoney war**, but then had to send them away again during the **Blitz**.

THE PROBLEMS

People in the countryside with a spare room were made to take an evacuee, but they could choose which one (smart, older girls went first, and boys big enough to help on the farm, then good-looking smaller children – and the ugly and the dirty were left till last). Sometimes brothers and sister were split up.

Some hosts found fostering an evacuee was deeply shocking:

• Some children did not know how to use a toilet, and urinated on the walls and on newspapers.
• Many poor children had lice and fleas.
• Bed-wetting was common.
• Some children swore and stole.

All evacuees were frightened and homesick at first, and worried that their parents would be killed in an air raid.

Some host households, also, were dreadful:

• Some hosts tried to make a profit out of the 50p a week they were given to look after the children.
• Some used the children as cheap labour.
• Some middle-class children ended up in filthy or violent households.

'I WEAR UNDERPANTS, DO YOU?'

But some children loved evacuation, and the fresh air, good food and adventure of country life. Some had never seen farm animals before, and got excited by events like Spring. One little boy went round telling all his friends: 'I wear underpants, do you?' Some of them came to love their new foster carers more than their own parents.

In some ways these children were more badly damaged by evacuation than those in bad homes, because they could not cope when they had to go back to London after the war.

CONSEQUENCES OF EVACUATION

Some historians believe that evacuation changed Britain. For many middle class families, it was the first time they had seen at first hand how poor some people were, and how poor people lived. Some simply blamed the children or the parents, but many people were shocked into believing that the government ought to give people a better standard of living after the war.

In this way, evacuation helped to create the **Welfare State** (see Chapter 24).

A SOURCE

In 1977 the historian Alan Jenkins wrote this about evacuation.

Many kind country people wanted to be foster carers, choosing children as they arrived. But then the problems started. The children would not eat cabbage and wanted to live on fish and chips. Some had never seen an egg and tried to bite it like an apple. Some could not tell cows from sheep.

B SOURCE

A government poster from 1940.

C SOURCE

The government let the newspapers show this picture of evacuees leaving by train.

D SOURCE

In 1986 the historian Peter Lewis wrote this about the effect of evacuation.

Some people thought it was a good thing that – for the first time – well-off people should see just how poor some people were.

Questions

a What does Source A tell you about the evacuation of children in 1940?

b Why were posters like Source B issued by the government in 1940? Use Source B and your own knowledge to answer this question.

c How useful is Source C to an historian studying evacuation during the war? Use Source C and your own knowledge to answer this question.

d Is Source D an accurate interpretation of the effects of evacuation on Britain during the Second World War? Use Source D and your own knowledge to answer this question.

Controversy!

'The government of 1939 ought to have been sent to prison for cruelty to children!'

What is your INSTANT REACTION?

Key Issue

- How fair was rationing?

Key Words
- rationing: butter, sugar, meat, tea, sweets
- register • ration cards • coupons • points
- alternatives: Dried Egg powder, Spam
  • British restaurants • Black Market
- Dig for Victory • healthier • Welfare State
  • Utility clothes, furniture

The aim of **rationing** was to stop prices shooting up and to make sure that everyone got a fair share of what food there was. The government was frightened that, without rationing, poor people would become angry and **morale** would fall.

During 1940 many items of food were put on ration – e.g. butter, sugar, meat and tea. Sweets were also rationed – you could have just 250 grams of chocolate a month (only five small bars, which meant that children's teeth were much healthier). By the end of the war, almost half the food items housewives bought were rationed.

People could not buy rationed goods where they wanted. They had to register with a shopkeeper. When they bought things, he stamped their ration cards and tore out the right number of ration coupons.

In November 1941, the government brought in a points system for food that was in short supply but not rationed. Every item was given a number of points, depending on how short supplies were (a big tin of salmon, for example, was 32 points, but a tin of tomatoes was only six). Each month, the housewife had 20 points to spend how she wanted. Housewives liked this – it put the fun back into shopping.

BEATING THE SYSTEM

People tried different ways to get round rationing:

1. They used alternatives – nettle tea, acorn coffee, Dried Egg powder (revolting) and fried 'Spam' (Supply Pressed American Meat **imported** from America – lovely!).

2. Many rich people simply ate out every night! This made ordinary people, stuck at home on rationed food, so angry that in 1942 the government ordered that hotels could not charge more than 5 shillings (25p) for a meal. It also set up 'British restaurants' which gave a good meal for less than the price of a packet of cigarettes.

3. The **Black Market** (buying things 'under the counter'). Most shopkeepers would set aside little extras for their favourite customers, and people were very nice to shopkeepers, especially butchers!

4. Dig for Victory. Many people started to grow their own food and keep pigs and chicken. The number of people with allotments almost doubled during the war.

Rationing worked so well that during the war the British people were better fed and healthier than ever before. This was especially true for poor people – and this was another factor that helped to bring in the **Welfare State**, because it made people realise how unfair society had been before the war.

UTILITY

Food was not the only thing in short supply. Petrol was rationed from the very start of the war. Wood and cloth were also in short supply.

After 1942, the government brought in **Utility** products. Women wore Utility suits (a one-piece trouser suit with a zip). And young newly-weds would buy utility furniture (for example, a cheap wooden wardrobe with a thin veneer and a cardboard back).

A SOURCE

A government poster about the shortage of cloth.

B SOURCE

A government poster about food shortages.

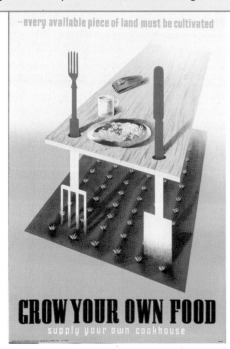

D SOURCE

In August 1941 an American journalist described the effect of rationing on British people:

There is no bad problem about food. On average, people's diet is as good as it was before the war.

Poor people in the towns are the worst-off, because they don't like vegetables, and poor people living in the countryside have come off best, because they can grow a lot of vegetables and keep a few chickens.

C SOURCE

In 2003 the modern historian Donald Thomas wrote this about rationing:

The government punished rich people who broke the law. Even so, ordinary people felt that the rich were not having to share the hardships everybody else was going through.

Questions

a What does Source D tell you about rationing in 1941?

b Why was Source B distributed in Britain during the war? Use Source B and your own knowledge to answer this question.

c How useful is Source A to an historian studying rationing? Use Source A and your own knowledge to answer this question.

d Is Source C an accurate interpretation of how rationing was viewed by the public? Use Source C and your own knowledge to answer this question.

Key Words
- conscription to the war industries
- munitions • 'nice girls' • dilution • pay
- 'shopping time'

'THIS WAR IS EVERYBODY'S'

In November 1939, the woman's magazine *Mother and Home* said:

The last war was a soldier's war. This war is everybody's.

What do you think it meant?

DID THE WAR CHANGE THINGS FOR WOMEN?

Historians disagree about whether the war improved the place of women in the workforce. Some evidence suggests that things changed a lot:

- After December 1941, women aged 20–30 could be **conscripted** to the women's armed forces (though not to fight).
- After 1941, women aged 18–40 could be conscripted to work in war industries; they could be told to go to any part of the country to work in any job the government wanted.
- The number of women employed rose from 5 million to 8 million in 1939–43.
- The number of women working in the **munitions** industry rose from half a million to two million.
- By 1943, nine out of every ten single women were doing war work.
- At first the government did not conscript married women, and women with children under 14 could not be sent away from home. After 1943, the government began to conscript married women as well.

DILUTION

However, there are some facts which suggest that things did not get better for women during the war:

- At first, few women volunteered for war work; the government had to introduce conscription in 1941.
- Women did not want war work, or to be sent away from home.
- There was a feeling that 'nice girls' did not work in factories.
- Some men workers did not want women workers, because they thought they would do their jobs for lower wages (this is called 'dilution').
- Women did not get equal pay, even if they were doing the same jobs as the men – even the government paid women less than men. Sometimes a woman in a skilled job got less than a man doing an unskilled job.
- The government did not provide enough nurseries, and mothers had to sort out their own day care for their children.
- Women in a full-time job found that all the shops were closed when they stopped work. They only got 'shopping time' if they were doing a 60-hour week. This was a big problem, because shopping was difficult enough in wartime Britain.

Even so, many women were glad to be able to help the war effort. Also, even though they were not paid as much as the men, women earned more than they had done. Before the war, the average women's wage was £2. During the war, women aircraft workers earned £5 a week and some women munitions workers earned £10 a week.

In 1989 Kay Ekevall remembered this about work in a shipbuilding firm during the war.

Women did most of the jobs – crane-driving, painting. I became a welder, but the men were paid more than the women. We had several battles over equal pay because we did the same jobs as the men. By the end of my time we had managed to get close to the men's wage.

A government poster asking women to help the war effort.

JUST A GOOD AFTERNOON'S WORK

PART-TIME WAR WORKER

Controversy!
'So women worked long hours for poor pay. Big deal! It was their men who were dying on the battlefields. The men were the REAL heroes of World War Two.'
What is your INSTANT REACTION?

One woman said this to Mass Observation in 1942.

Equal pay would upset the men. I like a man to have more money than me. I think it is twice as nice to have a dress bought for me by a kind man than to buy it myself, and this is because I am a woman.

In 1993 the historian Tim Healy wrote this about the effect of the war on women.

Many women enjoyed their changed lives, and the chance to earn wages, take on new challenges, and have new freedoms.

Questions

a What does Source A tell us about the role played by women in the war?

b Why did the government issue posters like Source B during the war? Use Source B and your own knowledge to answer this question.

c How useful is Source C to an historian studying the attitudes of women during the war? Use Source C and your own knowledge to answer this question.

d Is Source D an accurate interpretation of how the war affected women? Use Source D and your own knowledge to answer this question.

Write an essay on whether women's place in the workforce improved during the war, including:
• Evidence that some things improved
• Evidence that some things did not improve
• Your own conclusion

22 WOMEN IN THE ARMED FORCES

Key Issue

- How were women in the armed forces treated?

Key Words

- WRNS • WAAF • ATS • khaki • toilets
- jobs: secretaries, anti-aircraft gunners, cleaners, cooks, ferry pilots • discrimination

When women were **conscripted** in 1941, they were told they could join the WRNS (Women's Royal Naval Service), the WAAF (Women's Auxiliary Air Force) or the ATS (Auxiliary Territorial Service – i.e. the army). Most women wanted to join the WRNS because they liked the smart blue uniform – people of the time thought that army **khaki** 'is a colour every woman hates, and makes even a nice girl look common'.

In fact, women were told which service they had to join, and by 1944 half of the 450,000 women who had joined up were in the ATS.

'TOILETS WITH DOORS, PLEASE!'

Many women did not want to join the ATS. The ATS was the most dangerous of the services open to women; 335 were killed and another 300 wounded. ATS girls also had a bad name because it was said that they slept with the men. It is true that some ATS girls hated the army so much that they got pregnant on purpose so they would be sent home, but it is also true that fewer single women in the armed forces got pregnant than single women in other jobs. People at the time did not believe this, however, and many husbands and fathers did not want their wives or daughters to join the ATS.

Another reason that women did not want to join the ATS was because the toilets did not have doors. It did not bother the men, and nobody ever thought that the women might not like it!

Women were very important in the armed forces. They did work which let the men go to fight. They became mechanics and welders.

They also worked on the searchlights and the anti-aircraft guns. Some women served as 'ferry pilots' (they flew new planes from the factories to the airfields).

DOUBLE STANDARDS

Discrimination in Britain did not disappear because women joined the armed forces. Here are some examples:

- Most women who joined the armed forces were made to work as cleaners, cooks and secretaries.

- Women ferry pilots were not allowed radios in their planes, because RAF bosses thought they would gossip to each other.

- Women anti-aircraft gunners (who lived and worked alongside the men) were said to have sex with the men.

- Women who worked in the armed forces were expected to do hard and dangerous jobs, and yet be pretty and lady-like as well!

- Wounded women were treated differently to men. Diana Barnato, who served as a ferry pilot, said this: 'I always thought: "If I crash, I want to die". Men who lost an arm or a leg, or who were burned, were treated like heroes. But who would want to know a damaged woman?'

A SOURCE

In 1985 Joan Cowey remembered this about working with men on an anti-aircraft gun.

They said that all we were there to do was to sleep with the officers. The Americans were the worst: they said we were only there to 'keep the men happy'. They did not look at the work we did; everything they said about us just had to do with sex.

Full information
at the nearest recruiting centre
or your employment exchange

In Britain, many women did not join up because they heard stories about women soldiers behaving badly with the men.

Questions

a What does Source A tell us about attitudes to women in the armed forces?

b Why did the government issue posters like Source B?   Use Source B and your own knowledge to answer this question.

c How useful is Source C to an historian studying the role of women in the armed forces?   Use Source C and your own knowledge to answer this question.

d Is Source D an accurate interpretation of the problems faced by women in the armed forces during the war?   Use Source D and your own knowledge to answer this question.

C SOURCE

A painting by a British woman painter of WAAF women in Coventry learning to set up a barrage balloon.

Key Issue

• How far did the position of women really change?

WOMEN'S LAND ARMY

Before the war there were only 55,000 women farm workers, and male farm workers outnumbered them by 10:1. During the war, however, many men went off to fight, and 80,000 women joined the Women's Land Army (WLA) to take their place.

The WLA was a great success, but it was a hard job:

• Many farmers did not think the women would be able to do the job, especially as many of the women came from towns.

• WLA women had no say where they went or what they did. Many of them lived in poor conditions and had to go to the public baths for a proper wash.

• In 1944 WLA pay was only £2.40 a week and half of that went on lodgings (the average woman's wage was £3).

• They were accused of behaving badly.

WHAT CHANGED?

The war proved that women could do anything a man could do. However, the war did not change attitudes to women at work.

The war did not lead to more women having jobs. Many men did not like the idea of women going out to work. In 1943 there were 8 million working women – but by 1947 (after the war) this fell to 6 million, even though the government wanted women to stay in work.

In fact, many women left their jobs after the war because they wanted to. Some had delayed starting a family during the war, and left their jobs to have a baby.

Surveys in 1943 and 1947 found out that more than half the women of Britain believed that a married women should not go out to work.

Also, the war did not lead to women having better jobs. Skilled jobs were given back to the men returning from the war. Also, the government shut down many nurseries, so women had to leave their jobs to look after their children. Even by 1961, only 15% of doctors and only 4% of lawyers were women.

Did the war do much for women? This advert from the 1950s suggests that their real job was still 'homemaking'.

EQUAL PAY?

During the war, many women were angry that they did not have equal pay with men. In 1944 the government set up an investigation, which reported in 1946. It found that an average woman's wage was £3 a week, and an average man's wage was £5.70 a week, but it said that it could not do anything about this because their jobs were often slightly different.

By then the war was over anyway, and it was too late to make any changes.

RESPECT

The war had changed one thing. It had shown women that they *could* be equal. Many women had enjoyed working during the war.

So, after the war, many women went back to being 'homemakers' but, during the 1960s, when the women's rights movement started, they made sure that their daughters had the opportunities they had missed.

A SOURCE

In 1986 Mona Marshall remembered this about working in a steel factory:

The war was the best thing that ever happened to me. I was as green as grass and scared to speak to anyone. We had been taught to do as we were told – at work you did what your boss said and you went home to do what your husband said. The war changed all that. It made me stand on my own two feet.

B SOURCE

A 1942 photo of three girls in the Women's Land Army.

C SOURCE

Percentage of women in paid work:

	Single women	Married women	All women
1911	69	10	35
1921	68	9	34
1931	72	10	34
1951	73	22	35

D SOURCE

The modern historian Carol Harris has written this about the effect of the war on women.

During the war, everyone said that Britain's women were doing 'a man's job'. So when the war ended they were sacked.

Questions

a What does Source A suggest about how the war affected women?

b Why was the government keen to show Source B as an image of the Women's Land Army?

c How useful is Source C to an historian studying how the position of women changed as a result of the Second World War? Use Source C and your own knowledge to answer this question.

d Is Source D an accurate interpretation of how the war affected the position of women in society? Use Source D and your own knowledge to answer this question.

Make brief notes under the following headings:
- Women's Land Army
- Women's employment after the war
- Pay after the war
- Long-term change

Key Issue

- How did the war change life in Britain?

Key Words

- 1942: Beveridge report • Welfare State
- Clement Attlee: 'Let us face the future'
  Winston Churchill: communism, empire
- khaki vote • ranks • class • nationalisation
  • 1945 Labour government
  • end of greatness?

Winston Churchill had become Prime Minister in May 1940, when Britain seemed on the verge of defeat. He was a great war leader. He kept up Britain's **morale** during the difficult days, and he was ruthless enough to keep going until Hitler was completely defeated. The British people respected and followed him.

But, in July 1945, the British people voted him out of office. Instead they voted in a Labour Government by a landslide.

How did such an amazing turn-around come about?

THE BEVERIDGE REPORT 1942

After the beginning of the war, when things were going badly, the government knew that it needed to give the British people a reason to keep fighting. It had to offer them a hope for the future that would make it worthwhile carrying on the war.

In December 1942, therefore, Sir William Beveridge presented his report on Britain's Social Services. The Beveridge report was the basis of the **Welfare State**. It said that the government ought to provide:

1. A National Health Service that would provide free medical care (before the war, medical treatment had to be paid for, which was a great worry for poor people).
2. Good Council housing.
3. Unemployment pay and social security.
4. Good schools.
5. Full employment.

THE ELECTION CAMPAIGN

Churchill and the Conservative Party did not like these proposals and did not want them. During the 1945 election, Churchill was much more worried about the threat of **communist** Russia. But people did not want to hear about more trouble and the likelihood of a war with Russia – they wanted to know what was

This 1945 Labour election poster shows what people wanted – a new, better Britain, that would be worth fighting for.

going to be done about Britain's bombed-out houses, and what the government was going to do for them. Churchill said nothing about these things. Instead, he told voters that, if Labour won the election, they would bring in a British **Gestapo** to keep control of the people – this was a terrible insult to the Labour Party, and made people very angry, because during the war Labour had fought alongside the Conservatives to defeat Germany.

LABOUR: 'FACING THE FUTURE'

Churchill did not understand how the voters were feeling. Clement Attlee, leader of the Labour Party, knew what they wanted.

The Labour Party policy was called 'Let Us Face the Future'. Attlee promised to bring in the National Health Service and the Welfare State. He promised to build 4 million council houses for people who could not afford to buy a house.

In the election, Labour won 393 out of 640 seats in Parliament. The Conservatives only won 213. It was a huge victory.

THE KHAKI VOTE

It took three weeks before the people knew the result of the 1945 election. This was because people had to wait until the postal votes of the soldiers serving overseas (the '**khaki** vote') had been collected and counted.

This cartoon on June 1944, drawn by the cartoonist Vicky, shows that people were worried about what Britain would be like after the war.

These soldiers also voted in large numbers for Labour. Many of them resented their officers (as you can see from Source C), and they wanted a new Britain, which would be free of 'ranks' and 'class'.

1945: ALL CHANGE?

In 1945, the British people were proud to have won the war. They still felt that Britain was best. But they also felt that the victory gave them an opportunity to build a new, better Britain.

POWER TO THE PEOPLE

The historian Arthur Marwick said that the war changed Britain:

*During the war, many people came to believe that the government – which had organised industry so well to win the war – should keep control of industry after the war for the benefit of the people. The Labour government of 1945, therefore, **nationalised** coal, electricity and the railways.*

After the war, working-class people no longer accepted that the rich knew best, or that upper-class people ought to run the government. They had come to believe that they were equal.

The war led ordinary people to want more from life. They did not want to fight and die, only to go back to the slum housing, unemployment, poor food and poor health care they suffered before the war. They said that the wealth of Britain should give all people a good life, not just a rich few. They wanted a Welfare State that would look after the people of Britain 'from the cradle to the grave'.

BRITAIN IN DEBT

Not all historians think that the Welfare State was a good thing:

The historian Corelli Barnett said that the Welfare State was a mistake for Britain. After the war, much of Britain was ruined, and the country owed huge sums of money to America.

Barnett said that Britain should have spent the money on modernising industry, not on giving people benefits.

Some socialist historians have also said that the Welfare State was a bad thing. They say that the Labour Party's policies after 1945 were not very socialist, and that all they did was to put 'an acceptable face' on **capitalism** – keeping capitalism going, and not really changing the system.

THE END OF GLORY?

Britain won the Second World War, but many historians believe that the war was a disaster for Britain. They believe that the Second World War saw the end of Britain as a world power.

In 1945, Churchill had wanted:
- to keep Britain as a world power, and
- to defend the British Empire.

Churchill died in 1965. Huge crowds filed past his coffin and paid their respects to the 'man who got Britain through war'.

But by then, Britain had given away most of her Empire, and America and Russia were the two world powers.

Victory in the war and the 1945 election should have been Churchill's most glorious moment. Twenty years later, 1945 must have seemed more like the end of glory than its beginning.

A SOURCE

In 1985 the historian Paul Addison wrote this about the effect of the war.

It brought people together. They met in air raid shelters, in the tube stations and in the Home Guard, and when they queued for food. They talked to each other, and they wanted this spirit of friendliness to go on after the war.

This poster – showing a new health centre – was published by the British army in 1944. The government did not like the poster, and banned it.

YOUR **BRITAIN**

disease

FIGHT FOR IT NOW

Modern medicine means
the maintenance of good
health and the prevention
and early detection of
disease. This is achieved
by periodic medical
examination at Centres
such as the new Finsbury
Health Centre, where
modern methods are used.

ISSUED BY A.B.C.A.
DESIGNED BY F.H.J. ...

C **SOURCE**

In 1989 Frank Mayes, a British communist, remembered what happened when the sailors heard that Labour had won the 1945 election.

There was a big cheer, and one of the officers said: 'Well, I'm not going back to England'. So a sailor said: 'We will not miss you!' We all thought that Britain was going to be better and fairer. Of course it was not, and we were soon disappointed.

Make brief notes under the following headings:
• The Beveridge Report
• 1945 election campaign
• Labour's policies
• The khaki vote
• Impact of the war on Britain

D **SOURCE**

In 1986 John Beavan, editor of the *Daily Herald* newspaper (which supported Labour), remembered this about the war.

There was this feeling that everybody was working together, that everybody was doing something to help win the war – and that we were all equal.

Q**uestions**

a What does Source A tell us about how people remembered the war?
b Why was this poster issued in 1944? Use Source B and your own knowledge to answer this question.
c How useful is Source C to an historian studying attitudes among the British people in 1945? Use Source C and your own knowledge to answer this question.
d Is Source D an accurate interpretation of how Britain was during the war? Use Source D and your own knowledge to answer this question.

How to write about sources is as important in the exam as knowing what happened. You must practise this until you can do it.

EDEXCEL

The sources on which these examples are based are on page 3.

(a) *What can you learn from Source A about Churchill's views on the Munich Agreement? (4 marks)*

TECHNIQUE
- To get more than two marks for this question you must make an *inference* (i.e. 'read between the lines' to write something that the source *suggests* or *implies*).
- Two inferences with some explanation will get full marks.
- Start each idea with the same phrase each time: e.g. 'Source A suggests…'
- Example: *Source A suggests that the government had not stopped war coming, only delayed it, because it says: 'Do not think this is the end'. It also says that 'our defences are not good enough', which suggests that Britain would be at the mercy of Hitler if war broke out.*

(b) *Does Source C support the evidence of Sources A and B about* **appeasement**? *(6 marks)*

TECHNIQUE
- To get high marks, you must talk about *how much* the sources agree. It is a good idea to do this in a final sentence.
- Do not compare Source A with Source B. You will get no marks for this.
- Do not write about whether the sources are reliable or who wrote them. You will get no marks for this.
- Compare Source C with Source A, then compare Source C with Source B. Do not compare C with A and B together.

- Example: *Source C says that Britain had not re-armed, and this is supported by A where Churchill says that the government 'has not built up its armed forces in time'.*
  Source B, however, says the opposite, that 'Britain built up her armed forces during 1938–1939'.
  On the other hand, however, both B and C agree that appeasement was bad, B calling it 'a disaster', and C calling it 'cowardly'.
  On balance, C mostly supports A and B in that they all say appeasement put Britain in danger from Germany, although they disagree about the details of whether Britain re-armed'.
- Note the use of 'however'.
- Note the use of 'On balance' in the conclusion.

(c) *How useful are Sources D and E as evidence of the success or failure of the policy of appeasement? (8 marks)*

TECHNIQUE
- You must mention the *provenance* and purpose of the sources to get a high mark.
- all sources are useful for something, even if they are not reliable.
- Example: *Source D could be useful as evidence because it proves that many people supported appeasement at the time.*
  Source E is very useful, because it provides evidence that in the last year before the war 'Britain built up her armed forces' (as it says in Source B). Also, the figures come from a modern textbook, so we can believe them.

(d) *'Chamberlain's policy of appeasement towards Germany was the right policy at the time.' Use the sources and your own knowledge to explain whether you agree with this view. (12 marks)*

TECHNIQUE
- Don't just say whether you agree or disagree. First give the argument that suggests yes. Then give the argument that supports no.
- Don't go through the Sources one after the other. Group them into those which support the point of view of the question and those which do not.
- You don't have to mention all the sources, but make sure you write about most of them.
- Use both the sources and your own knowledge, or you lose half the marks. Flag up your own knowledge by starting the sentence with: 'From my own knowledge I know that…'
- Finish with a judgement. There isn't a right or wrong answer, but support your judgement by a short explanation.

- Example: *There are some sources that support this view. B and E show how appeasement gave Britain a year to build up her armed forces, and D and F show that many people agreed with appeasement at the time. However, other sources contradict this opinion. A, B and C all agree that appeasement was a disaster, that it gave Germany an advantage and put Britain in danger. In conclusion, I know that war broke out in 1939, so it is clear that appeasement failed to stop a war – it was a failure.*
- Do not use the words 'I think…'.

AQA

The sources on which these examples are based are on pages 10–11.

(a) *What does Source A tell us about the evacuation from Dunkirk? (3 marks)*

TECHNIQUE
- This is an easy question, and all you need to do is to provide three ideas – either bits of information from the source, or inferences (i.e. something the source suggests or implies).
- You will get no credit for adding knowledge of your own.
- Do not waste time by writing too much here.
- Example 1: *Source A tells us that the men had spent two days on the sand, that they joked and played games, and that one sailor's ship was sunk trying to rescue the soldiers.*
- Example 2 (an inference): *…It also suggests that the British morale was good because it says that the soldiers 'played games to keep their spirits up' and that the sailors were keen to save them.*

(b) *Why were photographs like Source B officially approved at the time? Use Source B and your own knowledge to answer this question. (6 marks)*

TECHNIQUE
- Use both the sources and your own knowledge. Flag up your own knowledge by starting the sentence: 'From my own knowledge I know…'.
- To get a high mark, you must give more than one reason.
- To get a high mark, you must mention the provenance and the purpose of the source.
- Example: *This photograph suggests that the British soldiers were still happy, and it shows a captured German gun. Yet I know that Dunkirk was a disaster and that the army lost huge amounts of equipment. The government showed photos like this because they wanted people to think that the war was not going too badly, that the men were in good spirits, and that Dunkirk wasn't all loss.*

I also know that the propaganda worked, because people still talk about 'the miracle of Dunkirk' instead of 'the disaster of Dunkirk'.

(c) *How useful is Source C to an historian studying the evacuation from Dunkirk? Use Source C and your own knowledge to answer this question. (8 marks)*

TECHNIQUE
- You need to make use of the source's provenance and purpose to score top marks.
- You should also test its usefulness by comparing it with your own knowledge.
- Don't confuse usefulness with reliability – a source can still be useful even if it isn't reliable.
- Example: *In some ways Source C might be useful because it shows the different kinds of ships that were used to pick up the men.*
However, it is a painting, not a photograph, so we do not know how factually accurate it is. Also, Wilkinson was an official war artist, and he painted this as a piece of propaganda to show the bravery of the British people, and to try to create the 'myth' of 'the miracle of Dunkirk'. So it is doubtful that this source is a reliable picture of an actual event.
This Source is more useful in showing us how the government wanted British people to think about Dunkirk, than what really happened.

(d) *Is Source D an accurate interpretation of the evacuation from Dunkirk? Use Source D and your own knowledge to answer this question. (8 marks)*

TECHNIQUE
- Don't just say whether you agree or disagree. First give the argument that suggests yes. Then give the argument that says no.
- You need to make use of the source's provenance and purpose to get a high mark.
- You should test the Source's usefulness by comparing it with your own knowledge.
- Example: *Source D says that the evacuation was a 'great success'. It says that the Germans failed to stop 'a third of a million men' coming home, and failed to capture many men. Also, from my own knowledge, I know that British morale kept up, Britain did not surrender, and went on to win the war.*
However, Source D does not say that the British had lost vast amounts of equipment. In addition, Germany had conquered France. Dunkirk was, in fact, a great defeat.
This interpretation is not accurate because it only tells one side of the story.
- Note the use of connectives like 'also', 'in addition' and 'however'.

GLOSSARY

Allied powers – the countries which fought against Hitler: Britain, America and Russia

Appeasement – the policy of giving Hitler what he wanted, in the hope it would prevent war

Aryan – the Nazi 'super-race' (i.e. 'pure', super-fit Germans)

Axis – the countries which fought against Britain: Germany, Italy and Japan

Black Market – the illegal sale of rationed goods 'under the counter'

Black propaganda – information designed to confuse and misinform the enemy

Blitz – the German mass-bombing of British cities

Blitzkrieg – a German word meaning 'lightning war' (see Chapter 3)

Capitalism – a system where the state allows private enterprise in business and private ownership of property

Censorship – where a government controls the media to stop people learning things it believes will damage morale

Communists – people who believe that the state should own the means of production

Conscription – where people are told to join the war or work in a war industry

Convoy – a group of merchant ships sailing together for safety

Democracy – a system of government where people vote their leaders into power at an election

Doodlebug – the V-1: a pulse-jet flying bomb

Eastern Front – the battle line between Germany and Russia

Evacuation – taking people from a place of danger to a place of safety

Fascist – extreme right wing (e.g. Nazis)

Fifth Columnists – people in a country who want the enemy to win

Gestapo – German secret police

Great Depression – economic depression, unemployment and poverty of the 1930s

Imports – the goods a country brings in through trade with other countries

Incendiaries – fire bombs

Infamy – shame, disgrace

Internment – imprisonment of suspected Fifth Columnists

Island-hopping – the American strategy in the Pacific (see Chapter 15)

Khaki – buff, sandy colour used for army uniforms

Lebensraum – a German word meaning 'living space'. The Nazis believed that they had a right to conquer eastern Europe because they were racially superior

Liberty/liberate – freedom/to free (from German occupation)

Looting – stealing from bombed shops and houses

Luftwaffe – the German airforce

Merchant ships – a ship carrying food or goods

Morale – the mood or spirit of the people

Mulberries – floating harbours designed for D-Day

Munitions – weapons, especially shells and bullets

Myth – a belief that is probably not true

Nationalisation – where the government takes over and runs an industry

Partisans – a civilian resistance fighter

Phoney war – the period September 1939–April 1940 when Britain was at war, but was not fighting Germany

Pre-fabricated – a method of construction where the parts are mass-produced in advance, and then joined together

Propaganda – where the media is controlled to make people think in a certain way

Rationing – fixing the amounts of food and goods people can buy to ensure a fair distribution

Raw materials – things (such as wool, iron and oil) needed by industry to make finished goods

Resistance – groups of civilians who fought against the Nazis occupying their country

Scorched earth – destroying everything before an invading army

Sitzkrieg – a play on the word Blitzkrieg, referring to a war where all you do is sit

Strategic bombing – using the airforce to attack enemy factories and towns

Tactical bombing – using the airforce to attack the enemy during a battle

Trekking – leaving towns to go and sleep in the countryside, away from the German bombing

Utility – cheap, sturdy clothes and furniture, which used as little cloth and wood as possible

Vengeance – revenge

Vichy France – the government set up by Hitler in France which collaborated with the Nazis

Welfare State – where the British government accepts the responsibility to look after the welfare of its citizens 'from the cradle to the grave'